"So much of what we know abou~~t Christ~~ narrative—either stories about Jesu~~s~~ Considering this, it is difficult to u~~nderstand~~ of understanding these Gospel stor~~ies~~ meanings is a formidable task for th~~em~~ from them chronologically, geograph~~i-~~ cally. In *The First Time We Saw Him*, Matt Mikalatos retains the scandal and surprise of the most famous Gospel narratives while recasting them in modern language that ignites the imagination and awakens the soul. This book will have you seeing aspects of the gospel anew and leave you wondering, 'Who wouldn't want to know a Jesus like this?'"

—**Jonathan Merritt**, author of *Jesus Is Better Than You Imagined*; senior columnist for Religion News Service

"Matt Mikalatos extracts the best-known stories of the Gospels from their ancient setting and inserts them boldly into a modern context. Here, biblical characters appear more vulnerable, immediate, and accessible. This is a must-read for Christians seeking a fresh look at the living, breathing Christ."

—**Josh D. McDowell**, author and speaker

"In this highly original book, Matt Mikalatos situates Jesus in contemporary settings with great insight and storytelling skills. In doing so, he ups the ante in our understanding of Jesus in ways that are unsettling, challenging, poignant, and inspiring all at the same time. No Christian will be able to remain complacent about his or her faith journey after reading this book."

—**Tom Krattenmaker**, contributing columnist for *USA Today*; author of *The Evangelicals You Don't Know*

"In *The First Time We Saw Him*, author Matt Mikalatos gives us Jesus in 3-D, the literary equivalent of viewing the Gospels on a giant IMAX movie screen instead of the tiny, cracked black-and-white television tubes of static images and stale imagination. But there are no camera tricks here, no spiritual special effects, because the truth as Matt shows us is clear, beautiful, and special enough already. Be warned, however. We'll be on the edge of our seats for this presentation, which shakes us out of our comfortable, preconceived ideas—just like Jesus did to everyone he encountered."

—**Clay Morgan**, author of *Undead: Revived, Resuscitated & Reborn*

"The Bible stories that should rock our world and corrode our naturalistic presuppositions often don't because of the twin barriers of all-too-familiar stories and unfamiliar culture. Matt Mikalatos retells some of those stories, placing them in today's world so we can feel the narratives and be refreshed by their life. As I read them, my professor's mind and pastor's heart were drawn to ponder anew the wonder of Jesus."

—**Gerry Breshears**, PhD, professor of theology at Western Seminary, Portland

"Matt Mikalatos has pressed the refresh button on the life of Christ, so that I felt the shock, relief, and even annoyance that Jesus's first audience must have felt. You'll find *The First Time We Saw Him* actually work on you with raw, subversive persuasion. A clever resource for any preacher, teacher, or small group wanting new ways to reveal Jesus's intelligence and surprising power."

—**Jonalyn Fincher**, vice president of Soulation

"Mikalatos has done it again: written a wonderful, insightful, and humor-filled book. Okay, that's not the full story. If I'm being honest, this blurb should read 'Mikalatos has done it again: written a wonderful, insightful, and humor-filled book that I WISH I WROTE!!!' Matt's contemporary 'retelling' of Sunday School's Greatest Hits breathes new life into the Bible stories we think we fully understand. Entertaining and smart, Mikalatos draws us closer to deeper understanding by meeting us where we live and telling the stories in a way that engages us here, now, in twenty-first-century North America."

—**Dan Merchant**, author of *Lord, Save Us from Your Followers*

"What if you could see Jesus like you've never seen him before? In a fresh way that shatters the complacency that comes from hearing the same stories so many times they barely reach your heart anymore? If you said, 'Yes! Bring it on!' then this brilliant collection of stories is for you. They opened my mind, but more importantly opened my heart, to the power of the gospel and the power of Jesus—not back then—but for today. I was completely captured by *The First Time We Saw Him*."

—**James L. Rubart**, bestselling author of *Soul's Gate*, *Memory's Door*, and *Rooms*

THE
FIRST TIME
WE SAW HIM

Other books by Matt Mikalatos

My Imaginary Jesus
Night of the Living Dead Christian

ADVENTURES OF VALIDUS SMITH

The Sword of Six Worlds

THE FIRST TIME WE SAW HIM

awakening to the wonder of Jesus

MATT MIKALATOS

BakerBooks

a division of Baker Publishing Group
Grand Rapids, Michigan

Published by Baker Books
a division of Baker Publishing Group
P.O. Box 6287, Grand Rapids, MI 49516-6287
www.bakerbooks.com

Printed in the United States of America

Library of Congress Cataloging-in-Publication Data
Mikalatos, Matt.
    The first time we saw Him : awakening to the wonder of Jesus / Matt
Mikalatos.
        pages cm
    ISBN 978-0-8010-1630-1 (pbk.)
    1. Jesus Christ—Parables. 2. Jesus Christ—Parables—Adaptations. I.
Title.
BT375.3.M55 2014
232.9'54—dc23   2013050260

The author is represented by Ambassador Literary Agency, Nashville, TN.

14 15 16 17 18 19 20   8 7 6 5 4 3 2

Contents

Introduction

One side effect of growing up in Christian culture can be a contemptuous familiarity with the Bible. I remember impatiently tapping my feet when we trotted out the Christmas story, begging for it to end so we could tear into the presents. I remember playing Bible Trivial Pursuit in sixth grade and thinking, *I know everything there is to know about the Bible, except how to pronounce some of the names.* But even the trivia of names seemed within my grasp. I knew that Mary's name in Aramaic, the language she spoke, was Miryam and in Greek was Maria. I knew that Jesus and Joshua were the exact same name in Hebrew, and that the name meant "God saves." I knew all there was to know, everything worth knowing.

I knew all the answers not because I had gone looking for them, but because they had been provided for me, like an answer key at the back of the book (or, more likely, in the margins and footnotes). There weren't questions I needed to wrestle with or even consider.

Over time the weight of all those flannelgraphs and picture Bibles and trivia games and cinematic portrayals and the occasional agenda-driven Bible study flattened Jesus out. It washed the color from the stories. Knowing all the answers made the Gospels little more than thinly disguised theological textbooks. I knew what would happen next and why and what that meant. Two-dimensional characters packed the Bible so tightly that I couldn't avoid them: the bumbling disciples, the evil Pharisees, the serene Christ.

Somewhere along the way my emotional responses to Jesus, which ranged from a mild, pleasant feeling all the way to a mild, semicrippling guilt, stopped matching the emotional responses of the people interacting with Jesus in the Scriptures.

The disciples felt terror when he calmed the seas.

The crowds experienced hate-filled, murderous impulses when they heard his teaching.

People wept in his presence. They repented of their sins. They fell at his feet in worship.

I started to wonder if maybe *I* was the simplistic, two-dimensional character. I needed to take a fresh look at Jesus.

However, taking a fresh look at Jesus presented a challenge, as if someone said, "Pretend you don't know English and learn it from the beginning." How do you do that? I'm still figuring that out. I've found invaluable help from church, from my friends and their disparate opinions about Jesus, and also from my time at seminary, where my professors pointed out that thinking I have it all figured out is a sure sign of ignorance.

We all hit that "I have it figured out" moment eventually. When our pastor takes the stage and says, "Turn to the story where Jesus says we must eat his flesh and drink his blood," we all sigh and turn there, already knowing what the sermon will be, maybe word for word. We're talking about Communion, or the Lord's Supper, and there's nothing shocking or upsetting about that, and we scratch our heads when some

of his followers leave Jesus because of his "hard teachings."
What's so hard about drinking grape juice?

What if we could find a way to make it all real to us again?
Let's talk about the Gospel stories in a way that might shock
us out of our preconceived notions and help us approach Jesus
with the same wonder, frustration, revelation, uncertainty,
and nervous fear that people did in the first century.

The retellings in this book of stories will be inaccurate, because, for example, finding an exact modern-day stand-in for
a Pharisee is impossible. If I say "churchgoers" for Pharisees,
the audience says, "Matt is saying churchgoers are evil." But
the Pharisees weren't evil, not in the black hat, gun-slinging
way we'd like to think. They were deeply spiritual, devout,
well-intentioned, and well-respected leaders in the community of faith, like our pastors, our seminary professors, our
teachers, and the people filling the pews on Saturday night
and Sunday morning. Pharisees would feel comfortable in
Christian culture, like it or not, which should make devout
Christians uncomfortable. I'm not saying churchgoers are
evil. I'm saying that Pharisees are more like us than different
from us.

These retold stories aren't literal translations, but that's
not their purpose. You likely have several "accurate-ish"
Bible translations sitting around your home. These stories
are meant to shake us out of our preconceptions, to give us
a jolt, to make us look at our dear, beloved, familiar Jesus
through new eyes. And while sometimes these retellings might
seem inaccurate, I'd encourage you to think of it like this:
If a child came up to you and asked you to explain what an
eight-track tape is, you could find an eight-track player and
buy it and show them how it worked. Or at some point you
might say, "It's like an MP3 player that only holds one album."
That's not accurate but it is insightful. It reveals the purpose

of the eight-track tape, to hold audio and entertain, much like an MP3 player. Some of the stories in this book are like that, inaccurate in some sense, but with the purpose of revealing an underlying truth through the simple process of connecting them to some common modern experience or context.

I pray that you will find these stories enlightening and that you read them aloud to your friends, perform them onstage, and share them at your church. I pray that they lead you to look carefully both at Jesus himself and the stories he told. Remember, the point is not to breathe new life into the Scriptures. It's to remind us that they're already alive.

1

The Past Is Prologue

She's sitting on the train, headed to her cousin's house. The rain beats on the windows, blurring everything outside to a green wash, and she's thinking it all through. From time to time she rubs her stomach and rests her head against the glass. She's devout, a follower of God. Sometimes following him means wandering into strange, unknown places, and this time she's scared. Her hands wander absently to the glass, her fingers tapping against the pane. A wave of adrenaline rises through her like a tide, and she takes a deep breath, trying to relax. She's scared. She's alone. She's in the dark.

She reminds herself that God's work often starts in darkness.

The holy words of Scripture say that when everything started, God's Spirit hovered over dark waters. Then God spoke and darkness rolled away, leaping over the waves, light chasing it to the farthest corners of the world. He spoke again and the empty void was filled with the sun and the moon, even the far reaches of emptiness gaining stars. Earth lifted up from the sea, and fish dove and spun in the water. Animals crawled on the ground, and birds flew with reckless joy through the brightly minted sky. Then God breathed into sculptured clay and created the seed of humanity. Even from the beginning she sees these themes: darkness replaced by light, emptiness filled, life where there was none.

But does that explain everything that has happened? She shakes her head, rubs her temples. She hopes Liz can make sense of it. Part of her says there's no room for doubt. She keeps mulling over what happened, her thoughts returning to it no matter what distractions she tries, and she's worried that she has been caught up in delusions of grandeur. It doesn't match what she thought before, how she understood God to work. She's no hero. That's who God uses, heroes. Not scared little girls. Her heartbeat speeds up at the thought; she can feel it booming against her chest. She takes a deep breath, filling herself.

That's how God is described throughout the Scriptures. As breath. As wind. As Spirit. God inspires, breathes into people, just as he breathed into that first human-shaped lump of clay. Her hand falls again to her flat, unchanged belly. God brings life wherever he pleases.

She thinks of all the times that the Bible says the Spirit "came onto" people, that he settled over them like a blanket. How about Saul? He was young, wasn't he? And the Spirit "came powerfully" on him and he spoke God's word to the people and later he became king. The stories of that Spirit and his interactions with the moving clay of humanity are full of people covered by the Spirit and becoming angry about injustice, speaking boldly about the truth, seeing the future clearly, standing up to perverted authorities. Prophecy, power, boldness, insight—there are these moments when God speaks into the world and interacts with humanity.

But still, that's nothing like what happened to her. She's not a hero or a prophet or a king. She's ordinary. She wakes up in the mornings in a room with posters of horses and a stuffed kitty on the pleated pink blanket, lined paper with her poems in purple ink crumpled on the floor, tacked to her walls, jumbled on her desk, and a minor obstacle course of strewn clothes stretching toward the closet. This is precisely where she stood in her sweatpants the color of the sky and her ivory tank top, her hair pulled loosely back, and her feet still in her slippers, when someone cleared his throat and said, "Good morning, most favored one."

Which sent her sprawling with a surprised yelp onto the floor and into her pile of laundry, her hair cascading into her face. She stared up at him through her veil of hair as he crouched down beside her and said, "God is with you."

She scrambled backward, confused. Not because he was in her room— she could tell with a glance that this wasn't an ordinary man—but because he called her *most favored one*. What could that possibly mean? That she was his favorite? The man's favorite? *God's* favorite? There's no way. Absolutely no way.

But the angel—that's what he was, an angel, to be sure—held up the palms of his hands and said, "No need to be afraid, Miryam. You've found favor with God."

He helped her to her feet and then, still holding her hands, leaned close and said, "Listen. You're going to get pregnant and you're going to have a baby boy. You'll name him Joshua. He's going to be a great man and he'll be called the Son of the Most High. God will make him a ruler, and he'll be over his people forever. There won't be an end to his authority, ever."

She could barely keep listening to him. Each new word, every new sentence brought questions careening into her mind. Get pregnant? How? She wasn't a child, she understood how it worked, but is that what the angel was saying? Her promise ring from Joe burned on her left hand at the thought. She didn't even have her driver's license yet; she wasn't ready for this. She wanted to wait to have kids. She wasn't even married, and now this angel was telling her she was about to get pregnant, and soon. And not just pregnant, but her son (her son!) would be a great ruler, a hero. Like in the Bible. She couldn't believe it and finally she looked at him and asked the question that was perplexing her the most, "How is this going to happen? I've never been with anyone."

The angel nodded and said, "God's Spirit will come onto you, and the power of the Most High will cover you." Like a cloud, its shadow falling across her. "So the holy child will be called God's son." And then, like an afterthought, "Your cousin Liz will have a baby too. Everyone said she couldn't have a baby, but she's six months pregnant. God does what he says he'll do, even if it seems impossible."

Liz. Her cousin, on her mother's side. Miryam didn't know all the connections and genealogies that led to making the old woman her cousin, but she was old all right, much too old to be having babies, and Miryam had heard nothing about it.

The angel stood there expectantly, as if he was waiting for something from her. What could she say after news like that? A thousand possible answers flooded her mind, a million questions, a billion little details bouncing around, trying to find a pattern that made sense. But in the end, despite all that, here were the facts: an angel stood in her bedroom with a message from God, waiting for an answer.

So she gave him one. What else could she say? "I belong to God. All those things you've said, if that's the plan, I'm on board."

And then the angel left her alone in her room, the stuffed kitty fallen over and watching her with one button eye. He left her without a word of how to explain this to her parents, to her boyfriend, to the kids at school, to the priest. What would she say? "I'm pregnant with God's baby"?

That conversation didn't go well with Mom and Dad. They didn't believe her, didn't even believe she was pregnant. Her father actually laughed and pulled her close, tousled her hair. Her mother watched her without blinking, her eyes narrowing. In the end, Miryam couldn't bear to say anything to Joe but she walked to the corner convenience store and bought a rectangular box she snuck into the house, into the bathroom, and she sat there, staring at the test, waiting, and the small blue cross slowly appeared, bright and certain and shining like a star.

So now she's on the train, on her way to see Liz. Her mother thinks it's a good idea, that Miryam will see what it's like to have a baby, that she'll stop talking nonsense. Miryam knows that's not going to happen. She's going to speak nonsense if that's what God speaks to her and, yes, she understands that this is hard to believe. She's struggling to believe herself, to keep herself from buying another pregnancy test at every convenience store she passes. She didn't ask for a sign, she didn't ask for proof, because she thinks that an angel appearing in one's bedroom is proof enough.

But the angel gave her a sign anyway. He said Liz was pregnant. Old Liz. And it is with her heart hammering in her chest that she walks up the cracked sidewalk toward Liz's house, leaning sideways with her duffel bag banging against her legs. She knocks and waits for a few minutes, but Liz and her husband, Zach, are old and must not have heard. Although no one tells her to enter, she pushes the door open.

Zach is sitting in an ancient leather chair, his white hair standing at comical angles and reaching out to her like his arms, the arms that wrap her close to his thin chest. He doesn't say a word. Miryam says hello, that she's happy to see him, and then there's a surprised cry from deeper in the house, somewhere near the kitchen.

Liz comes bustling out, her apron on and sleeves rolled up and flour on her arms and chest, her flyaway hair pulling loose from its bun and giving her a wild silver halo. She wraps Miryam in her fleshy arms, the firm bump of her belly pushing against Miryam's, and she practically shouts, "Oh, you are a happy woman! And the baby you're going to have, he's happy too!"

Liz holds her at arm's length, and Miryam can see tears in the corners of her eyes when she says, "But what's so special about me? Why am I favored so much

18

that the mother of my Lord should come here to me? As soon as I heard you say hello, my baby jumped for joy!" Liz throws her head back and laughs, Zach standing behind her, a silent grin on his face. Liz yanks her close again, belly to belly, Miryam's face cradled against Liz's shoulder, Liz's one hand stroking Miryam's hair, the other circled around her. "You'll be happy, Miryam. You've believed the promises God has spoken to you."

And she did believe! Any last doubts drain away in the arms of the old pregnant woman. Her shoulders relax, her heartbeat slows, her hands unclench. She relaxes into her cousin's embrace and she can feel Liz's baby under the apron, kicking. No, not kicking. It is more than that: it's a drumbeat, a dance, a whirling, ecstatic motion from Liz's stomach and against Miryam's, as if Liz's baby wants to get to hers, as if these little cousins want to embrace too. He is leaping in there, jumping for joy. Miryam puts her palm against Liz's belly and whispers hello. She closes her eyes and lets the baby's excitement wash over her. A smile pulls at the corners of her mouth. She's ready, she thinks. Come what may, she's ready.

God's Dream Team

Every once in a while my kids like to hear their birth stories. My eldest, Zoey, was born in a hospital in Seattle, with Dr. Neighbor and his best friend, Dr. Jokey, doing the honors. Dr. Neighbor was deadly serious and Dr. Jokey was a non-stop series of one-liners, dressed in scrubs and a face mask. When Zoey was born, they wrapped her up in a pink blanket that said "Welcome to the NEIGHBOR-hood" (no doubt Dr. Jokey's influence) and handed her over.

The big surprise when Dr. Hickerson handed me my second daughter, Allie, was when the nurse said she was a redhead. Since my wife has light brown hair and I have black hair, we were skeptical. But that first bath revealed gorgeous red hair. This gave rise, eventually, to a favorite family moment when a brown-haired waitress asked three-year-old Allie, "Where did you get that red hair?" and Allie looked at her like she was crazy and said, "God gave it to me." And then, after a moment's reflection, "That's where you got your hair, too."

I don't recall the name of our doctor in Vancouver, Washington, who delivered our youngest daughter, Myca. But I do recall that his job before becoming a doctor and coming to America (he was Australian) was as a veterinarian in the Outback (of Australia, not the steak house). He did a one-man C-section that took, and I am not exaggerating here, maybe ninety seconds from first cut to, "Here's your baby." G'day, mate!

For sweet baby Jesus, the story was longer and more complicated and, let's face it, a little weird. It's a story that's important enough and strange enough that many cultures celebrate it annually at Christmas. My mom made a birthday cake for Jesus every year, and we sang "Happy Birthday" by the heavily ornamented tree. One of the most baffling things about the Christmas story (a story full of strange things) is that God did things differently than he had up to this point.

For some context, here's a quick biography of the Holy Spirit. The Holy Spirit is God and is often the person who takes the front line in communication with human beings. It's interesting that the word *spirit* in both Greek and Hebrew (the languages in which most of the Bible was written) can mean spirit, breath, or wind. Often the words we use to describe the Holy Spirit and how he interacts with us are metaphors. He fills people. He directs them "like a wind." He descends "like a dove." Metaphors are illuminating but not always precise, something that's helpful to remember as we take a quick spin through the Spirit's interactions with humanity.

He was hanging out before the creation of the world. The Bible says the Spirit of God was hovering over the waters in darkness when he decided it was time to create the universe we know and love. So he declared, "Let there be light."

Darkness. Water. Emptiness. God's Spirit in the midst of that. And at his words, creation came into being—because God said so. Then God said, "Let us make humanity in our own image." So he did. The Bible says that God formed "the Adam" out of the ground, that he sculpted him, and then breathed (spirited) the breath (spirit) of life into his nose, and the Adam became a living soul.

Then for thousands of years, we see the Holy Spirit showing up and interacting with human beings in fascinating ways. Isaiah 63 implies that when the great wind (spirit?) comes and separates the Red Sea so God's people can walk across on dry land, it happens because the Holy Spirit had been "set among" his people.

When God sets his people to the task of building objects of worship, the Holy Spirit gives a man named Bezelel wisdom, understanding, knowledge, and skills for the task. The Holy Spirit inspires (breathes into) Bezelel.

The Bible describes the Holy Spirit when he "comes onto" people. He rests on them like a cape, giving them power. In fact, a young man named Saul has the Holy Spirit "come powerfully" on him and he starts to prophesy, to speak for God. Later he becomes the first king of Israel.

It's a pattern that continues for thousands of years. The Holy Spirit comes upon people, empowering them, making them angry when they should be angry, giving them courage to speak truth or strength to fight enemies. These people tend to be special people. Prophets and prophetesses. Kings and queens. God's spokespeople. All along the way, these prophets and spokespeople keep making promises for God (or God makes promises through them if you prefer). Promises about someone who will put an end to all the suffering in the world. Someone who will save us. Someone who will make us more like God. There are different words used in the Bible for this person. The *Savior*. The Jewish people called him the *Messiah*. The Greeks called him the *Christ*. But every follower of God knew this: someday, the savior of the world would come and explain everything to us and show us the way to be with God forever. That's precisely what Miryam is waiting for, along with all the devout followers of God.

So after all these centuries, an angel finally shows up and says, "At last the time has come." This is the turning point in human history, the thing we've all been waiting for. And now it's time for God to build his dream team. So he chooses an unmarried but devout virgin girl from a backwater town. He picks a devout priest, who thinks his prayers for a child have been useless, and his elderly wife, who lives in shame because she has never borne children. He chooses an unborn baby named John, and a carpenter whose fiancée is suddenly pregnant and not by anything he's done. Then he picks an old man and an old woman at the temple and a handful of shepherds and some astrologers. I suppose Joseph's donkey was part of the team too.

Everything has changed. Now, instead of empowering prophets and kings, the Holy Spirit impregnates a young girl. Elizabeth hears Mary's voice when she walks into the house, and the Holy Spirit comes on her—on Elizabeth, the priest's wife, not a prophet, just an old lady who can't have babies. Then the Holy Spirit tells the unborn baby John, "Hey, baby Jesus is in the room," and John starts to dance in Liz's womb.

From the very beginning, this baby, this savior, God in the flesh, did things differently. For those who have grown up in Christian circles, we take the story for granted. It's the story we read before we open gifts, and we all wait impatiently for the last word so we can tear open the colored paper and find out what surprises wait inside. A new computer? A book I've wanted? Frankincense? Myrrh?

A Christmas Story

The real surprise, the first of many, is that God chose to do it this way. Soon after I graduated from college, I had a chance to visit an underground church in a closed country in Asia. A "closed country" is one where the nation's laws about religion make Christianity illegal in some sense, and an underground church is one that meets illegally, in secret. This church was made up of recent converts to Christianity, mostly college students, who had been believers for less than a few months. I sat next to a young girl, a follower of Jesus for six weeks, as we played a silly Christmas game.

It was one of those dumb plays, where people at the party take on the roles of the Bible story, and you read it aloud while people act it out. One student played the part of Joseph, and another the angel. A third played Mary, and another got on all fours to portray the donkey. A sofa cushion shoved under a shirt played the part of infant Jesus. It was the sort of eye-rolling Christmas activity I had grown accustomed to in my many years of Christian living.

Except the girl next to me, the young Christian, had never heard the Christmas story. Her eyes lit up when the angel appeared and she said, "How wonderful! An angel came!" She looked perplexed at the idea of Mary giving birth without having sex. She grinned through the whole journey to Bethlehem and the miraculous birth in the stable. The star! The shepherds! The wise ones from the East! (She smiled. She was from the East too.)

She looked at me at the end of the story, and I realized I hadn't been watching anymore, that the tiny play in front of us had changed somehow, from an eye-rolling piece of cheesy Christian theater into something profoundly moving and beautiful because I was watching the story reflected in this young woman's face. She looked at me and said, "Why would he do that? Why would he come as a baby? He didn't have to do that."

Her words hit me in the chest. It had never occurred to me that God might have chosen to do things another way. I had known this story, that God had become a human being—that he had come as a baby—since I had been a baby myself.

Why would he do that?

Why didn't he just come as a king?

As an adult?

Why let himself be poor?

Why be born to someone with no influence?

I didn't have a single answer for her. Why would God, the greatest being in the universe, choose to be born in a backwater, occupied country in the far corner of the world's mightiest empire? Why choose an unmarried couple to be his parents in a town where they didn't have a bedroom or a crib? Why would the almighty God allow himself to be born into a place of poverty, weakness, vulnerability, and lack of influence?

Why, in other words, would God choose to become so much like me?

24

No More Darkness

Certainly these questions must have occurred to Miryam over the years, because there was so much more to come, more than just being told that her baby would be the savior, that he was God's son. There she is, lying on the fold-out sofa at Liz's house, thinking over all that has happened: the amazing story Liz told her about Zach being unable to speak after questioning his own angelic messenger, and how they knew that the baby in Liz's womb would be named John, just like Miryam knew that hers would be Joshua.

She pulls a lined notebook out of her duffel bag, rustling around with one hand for a pen, and she starts to write a poem. It's how she thinks, how she remembers, how she prays. She writes and crosses out lines and scribbles in the margins with arrows showing where newly added words should go. In the end she slumps into sleep. She doesn't notice when Zach comes and gently pulls the purple pen from her slackened fingers and smoothes the crumpled paper on the kitchen table before puttering through the house and turning out all the lights.

> The Lord is amazing! Everything in me
> Says it. My breath exploding
> With the thought of the God who saves.
> He has been watching me, his slave,
> He has been aware of my lowly place.
> From this day on all who see my face
> Will say, There's a happy woman,
> No doubt she could write a sermon
> About the things he's done, about his name

Which deserves respect, which demands acclaim.
He's quick to forgive and his patience is long
For those who respect him, and his arms are strong.
Proud people run when they see him flex.
He has deposed kings, thrown down presidents.
He takes the lowly, the humble, the outcast
And gives them a title that will always last.
He fills the stomachs of the poor with food.
Only the poor! The rich are excluded.
He always helps Israel, his servant.
Going back to Abraham, our God is not absent.
He remembers to forgive us for all our ways
Because he promised to do it and he does what he
says.

She wakes in darkness, a darkness so deep that she can't see the ceiling and she almost laughs at the thought, because there is no darkness, not anymore. She thinks of the old words, "The people walking in darkness have seen a great light." She thinks of her own emptiness and rubs her belly again. Joshua is in there, somewhere, as small as a piece of gum. Her empty womb, filled. Life where there was no way for life to come into being. He is light in her darkness. He is filling her emptiness. He is life where life is not possible.

One day soon, not even nine months from now, she will think of this again. Joshua will be born in that attached garage, Miryam on an inflatable bed, her hair pasted by sweat to the side of her face. Joe will take a long, red toolbox and remove the screws from the lid. He will dump out the tools on a workbench, and she will wrap Joshua in a blanket, wrap him tight and place him inside it, near her bed. Somehow in the night he'll wriggle his tiny hands loose and she'll reach to him, and his tiny twig-like fingers will clutch her pinky. The savior of the world, and he can't get his hand around her finger. The star will wash the whole garage with blue light, and as his miniscule lips smack together, his chin pushing forward, rooting for her breast, she'll pull him close and ask herself: *What sort of man will Joshua be? The son of God, yes. The savior of the world, yes. A tiny, helpless infant, her son, yes, yes.*

But what sort of man will he be? Who is he?

And the star will say he is the light.

Her heart will tell her he is fullness.

And the tiny, speeding motor of his heart will remind her that he is life.

And they will lie back, sweating together on the inflatable bed, and sleep.

2

Lost

In college I invited one of my friends to go to church with me. She had black-dyed hair with purple streaks and a habit of wearing short leather skirts with tall leather boots. And a dog collar. And she had various piercings. So maybe I shouldn't have been surprised when we were asked to leave. She was humiliated. I was furious. She wasn't "dressed appropriately for church," because when we go to church, we should be squeaky clean. We should be dressed in our "Sunday best." We should look like the other people in the pew. I guess I should have asked her to take the dog collar off and pull out the piercings and put on a floral-print dress, but honestly it didn't occur to me. I didn't think it was necessary.

Sometimes when we talk about people who are "lost," we say it in a derogatory way. We say it like they wandered off the map and can't be bothered to stop for directions. Or they've "lost their moral compass" and they're off doing wrong things because they're too depraved or too stupid or too selfish to do the right thing.

That's not how Jesus talked about the lost though. Not at all. In fact, he had all sorts of friends who wouldn't be welcome in church. He would hang out with them at bars and go to their parties, and it didn't make people happy with him. He was a religious teacher, and people expected him to live up to a certain standard. He shouldn't be hanging out with the junkies and the sex-trade workers. He should be with the church folk.

The fact is that sometimes Jesus smells like stale cigarettes. The stench of spilled booze and musk and marijuana clings to him with an apologetic shrug, the side effect of hanging out with alcoholics and tweakers and whores and johns. When the fresh-faced, fresh-scrubbed, freshly dressed church people come awkwardly into the room, like children into a haunted house, startled and scared and disbelieving, the question they always ask without thinking or remorse is, "Why?"

Why are you spending time with these people?

Why aren't you bricking them off in their section of town?

Why aren't you staring past them on the sidewalk and hoping for the walk signal?

Why aren't you locking the car door and trying not to make eye contact?

A Trip to the Zoo

Joshua pulls his tangled hair out of his eyes and smiles reassuringly at the church folk who have searched for him and found him here. Over the thrumming bass of the house band, he begins to tell a story.

Andy was a second-grade teacher in downtown Los Angeles. The poverty of Andy's students made a knot in his stomach, and he thought of them almost as his own children, although he didn't have any, which was okay, because some of them didn't have a father.

Andy worked hard to give those kids some fond, Technicolor memories, so that as adults they could think back on their childhood without nightmares. One year he hatched a plan for a field trip to the San Diego Zoo, complete with pictures in front of the giraffes and taking home stuffed tigers and ice cream cones melting all over seven-year-old fingers.

The school didn't have the money budgeted, of course, and the children didn't have any, and Andy certainly didn't, but he made phone calls and begged administrators and wrote politicians and cajoled zoo employees until he scraped together enough promises and permissions to fill a long yellow bus full of volunteers and second graders—not just his own class but every second grader in the school—and ride down to the best zoo in the world.

He put them on the buddy system and assigned them to clusters of ten with an adult in each and he marched them proudly through the parking lot and past the ticket booths and then off to the polar bears. The kids laughed and one kid said, "What about the penguins?" And Andy said, "Not yet. Stick together, and grab your buddy. Stay with your partners."

He counted the kids often: . . . *96, 97, 98, 99, 100.* He kept them from climbing on fences, snagged wanderers, and picked up little Selina when she turned her ankle and couldn't keep up.

He counted to a hundred at the giraffe enclosure, at the monkey environment, at the sea lion tank. He counted to a hundred more times in one day than his students had all year and he smiled at the thought. At lunch he counted again: . . . *96, 97, 98, 99—no number 100!* Maybe one of the kids had switched tables. He counted again: . . . *97, 98, 99.* His heart beat faster, his teeth clenched, and he pointed at each of them now as he counted: . . . 97, 98, 99.

He put out the zero call to the kids, the sign for them to take their volume down to nothing and sit quietly, and when the children were sitting still with their half-eaten sandwiches and cracker bags in front of them, he counted one more time. Roger Hom was missing. Roger. A good, well-behaved, but curious kid. Andy wasn't surprised he had wandered, just surprised he had gotten away. So what did Andy do? A mathematician might shrug his shoulders and say, "Aw, what's one kid more or less?" He still had 99 percent of his students. He could write off that 1 percent.

No! Of course not, not Andy. He arranged the parents in a perimeter around the kids and he drew an imaginary circle around them and said, "Listen, if these kids cross this line, tell them to get back over it, because this is public school and that's all we have the authority to do."

He raced back through the zoo, past the lions and giraffes and monkeys, grabbing every person he saw and shouting, "Have you seen this kid, seven years old, about this high, answers to Roger?"

He told the zoo staff and the concession workers and the passersby and he scoured every square inch of that zoo until finally he found Roger, safe and sound, looking placidly at the penguins. Andy scooped him up into his arms and squeezed him so hard that Roger looked at him with a warm and happy confusion. Andy put Roger on his shoulders and marched back to the rest of the class. When he came into view of the wall of parents, they let out a ragged cheer.

Joshua clears his throat and takes a small sip from his water bottle and says, "In the same way, there is more cheering in heaven about one lost child coming home than for the ninety-nine who stayed in the right place."

Precious

Why did Jesus hang out with the broken people? Because "the lost" are precious to God. In the same way that Andy wouldn't shrug and say, "What's one student, more or less?" Jesus doesn't leave one of his own. In Luke 15 the parable is a story about sheep. Ninety-nine still in the pen, one lost, and the shepherd leaves the ninety-nine to save the one. I never understood that. I thought, *Why risk the majority to save one little lamb?*

According to my friend Dr. Mary, people in the Middle East understand this immediately. Dr. Mary did medical missions in Pakistan for over twenty years. She tells this story about an old woman who had come into the hospital. And somehow, someway, this old Pakistani woman got into a conversation with one of the doctors about the Christian God. The doctor explained, "Here is a story about how God feels about you. Once there was a shepherd who lost one sheep but had ninety-nine safe in the pen."

And the old woman said, "Ah! So the whole village formed a search party and went to look for it."

"Yes. They left the ninety-nine safely behind, and the shepherd went to look for the one lost lamb. And when he found it—"

"They had a great celebration in the village!"

"Yes. And that is how God feels toward each of us. Jesus said, 'There is more rejoicing in heaven over one sinner who repents than over ninety-nine who did not need to repent.'"

The old woman started to cry and said, "What a wonderful story. You mean that God feels that way about me?"

"Yes," the doctor said, and the old woman immediately moved the curtain beside her bed to tell the people who shared the room the wonderful news she had just heard.

The lost are precious to God.

The Old Woman Who Almost Loses It

After Joshua finishes his story, someone—a woman in a floral-print dress, maybe—starts to say something, and her lips have been pressed together so hard they've lost their color, and the angry crease between her eyebrows hasn't relaxed this whole time. Before she gets a word out, he raises his hand and says, "I'm not finished."

Then with a faraway look in his eyes, he starts another story.

One afternoon Rosalba Arvisu, who lives in a broken-down apartment not far from Andy's school, opens her mailbox to find a thin, cream-colored envelope. A note from Humberto spills out, and it says, *Abuelita, para ti.* She spreads out the contents of the envelope on her round, pockmarked kitchen table and fans out the five bills. She hasn't had five hundred dollars in her hand in a long, long time.

She says a prayer for her dear Humberto, working up north on some rancher's land. He is a kind and generous man, who not only pays well but provides housing and sometimes even food, praise God. Rosalba says a prayer for the rancher too and she crosses herself and asks God to bless that rancher who is generous enough to Humberto that her grandson can send enough money to melt her heart with kindness. She suspects he has sent her more than he has kept for himself.

She puts the bills carefully back into the envelope and holds it for a while, smiling, one hand on the envelope, the other resting over her heart. Then she takes the bills out again, stacks them beside the sugar bowl, and throws away the envelope.

She busies herself cleaning the apartment, because even though the complex is falling apart year by year, that's no excuse for her own home to fall apart. She makes a pot of beans, and when she comes back to the table, she counts only four bills. She looks on the floor around the table. She moves the cracked flower vase, she shifts the chairs around and looks in the seats, she looks under the sugar bowl, and then in a strange afterthought, she lifts the lid—you never know.

She hurries down the stairs to the mailboxes, scanning the floor as she goes. She grabs one of the neighbors, Mrs. Hom, and asks her if she's seen it. She knocks on the door of the boys who live down the hall, the ones who are so poor that they rotate sleeping in the bunk beds while the others are off at work, as if they were sailors in a submarine. They haven't seen the money.

At last she goes back to the apartment and methodically searches the bathroom and the bedroom, even though she hasn't let even her shadow into those rooms since the money arrived, and at last—just as desperate sobs are choking their way through her chest and she's saying to herself, *Be strong, Rosalba; be strong, old woman, you will find it*—she reaches into the wastebasket for the thirtieth time and looks in the envelope for the sixtieth, and there it is, the most crumpled, torn, beautiful slip of green paper she has ever seen, stuck to the envelope it had come in.

When she finds it, she lets out a whoop of joy, her hand fluttering to her heart. She falls onto a kitchen chair, her legs kicked wide, and the soles of her feet facing the oven. When she recovers, she makes an enormous batch of her famous tamales, then races around the apartment complex, inviting everyone to come and celebrate. They pack into her kitchen, the Homs and old Mr. Pattison from next door and those boys down the hall, who eat more than their share, which warms her heart and makes her feel for one moment like Humberto's kind rancher, and she packs their arms full of leftovers when they leave.

When he finishes, Joshua looks at the woman in the floral dress, and now her arms are folded across her chest, but a bit of color has come back into her lips and maybe, just maybe, she's starting to feel what he's saying. He looks her right in the eyes and says, "It's like that. God's people throw a party to celebrate one crumpled, torn, used-up sinner who turns away from her old life and comes home to God."

We've all lost something important. A credit card. A check. A birth certificate. We've torn apart our apartments and houses and glove boxes trying to find something we've lost, trying desperately to recover it, racking our brains over where we left it. And Jesus says, "There is rejoicing in heaven over one sinner who repents." Because the lost are valuable to God.

3

Frank Chases His Dreams
in Hollywood

When the teacher finishes telling them about the lost kid and the missing money, people still look at him in consternation.

"Really? That's the reason you're hanging out with drug dealers? Because an old lady found some lost pocket change?"

The teacher looks at the fresh-faced people from the right side of the tracks. Anger, confusion, frustration. One of them snaps that they want a straight answer. His wife shushes him, and a small conference breaks out off to the right. Just when he thinks that might end it, that they will walk away, thinking about his stories, mulling them over in their minds, and arguing among themselves what they might mean, one of the pagans to his left finishes rolling his joint, hangs it on his bottom lip, and lights it with a casual elegance, shaking out his match and taking a deep drag. One of the spiritual people frowns as if to say, *See? This is what we're asking. How can you sit there while some kid smokes pot next to you?*

The kid offers Joshua a hit and, like always, he waves him off. He feels the weight of the churchgoers' eyes, daring him to say something. A man reknots his tie, waves the smoke from in front of his narrow face, and coughs. The teacher smiles, takes the joint from his friend, and crushes it out in the yellowed ashtray. He gives his friend a meaningful look, and the kid looks at the strangers, looks at the teacher, and shrugs, tucking the snuffed-out joint into his jacket pocket for later. The teacher leans his elbows on the table behind him and crosses his ankles and tries one more time.

As the words spill from him, they all lean closer: the church people and the not-yet-church people, all united in their desire to hear the story, to understand what Joshua is saying.

It's like this kid named Frank, who only ever wanted to be an actor. His father was a farmer and his older brother was a farmer and his father expected him to do the same thing, but Frank couldn't bear the thought of that and sometimes he stopped a combine in the middle of a far field and got out of the cab and walked through the wheat and quoted Hamlet to himself. More than once he saw the dagger before him and wondered if it was meant for his father or for his dreams of acting.

His father tried to get Frank's head off the stage and into the fields, and they had spectacular fights that ranged for acres.

Frank would ask his father, "Don't you care about my dreams? Don't you want me to succeed?"

His father, frustrated and dusty and sun worn would turn his leathered face to his son and wonder how it was possible that this was his boy. He couldn't find the words to answer him. Every sentence led down a different road but they all arrived at the same place, with Frank angry and unsatisfied. One day in the middle of a particularly unpleasant fight that had sent Frank's brother out of earshot with a smug smile on his face and the hired hands looking for other corners of the ranch to work, Frank's father realized that the boy was asking about money.

At last he snapped, "Son, when I die you can use my money to do as you please."

And Frank yelled, "I wish you were dead right now!"

The words hung over them like a morning mist, and Frank's father closed his eyes, hoping the sun could burn them away but it didn't and it couldn't. He could hear Frank panting beside him, could hear even his fists clenching and unclenching and he said, "You don't mean that."

But when he said it, his voice sounded old and as brittle as a husk of wheat, and for a moment he understood why his son hated him. "You don't mean that," he said again, but quietly, almost to himself.

Frank did mean it, though, or at least enough that he didn't try to take back the words hanging between them, and the next morning Frank was pleased to see that his father had put a for-sale sign on half the property. Frank told himself that this meant his words had done their work, and it wasn't but three months later that Frank was a millionaire and on his way to Los Angeles to make his way in the world without so much as an apology. He left an awkward good-bye note on the kitchen table before his buddy picked him up and drove him past his father's fields and then the fields that used to be his father's fields and finally to the airport.

Being young and single and rich, he found it easy to make friends. He went to a couple of casting calls and met some struggling actors and some low-level producers or wannabe directors and almost got an agent. He threw lavish parties in his spectacular rented home and picked up his growing stable of friends in his yellow Porsche. His parties grew to ridiculous proportions and included prostitutes and drugs and whatever else they could find to pass the nights in pleasure, and soon enough his house smelled like marijuana and smoke and spilled booze and sex. That lasted a good long while. Years.

With all the parties and sitting by the pool and spending money, Frank hadn't made much progress toward an acting career or a career at all, and one morning he came running out his front door, his silk robe snapping around his thighs because someone was breaking into his car. It wasn't a thief though, it was a repo man. Frank had fallen behind on his payments a couple of months before, and he kept telling the credit agency he'd pay soon. He had every intention of doing that and he started calling in debts and then favors and then welfare.

When the money ran out, so did Frank's friends. He got evicted soon after he was busted for buying a dime bag off an undercover cop, which made it harder still to find a job, and eventually he found himself on the sidewalk with a duffel bag and fifty bucks, broke and broken.

He moved into a dilapidated apartment building with five other guys, rotating through the beds depending on who had a shift at work, and still he was barely able to pay his share of the rent. He watched the blue and red lights on the ceiling of his room, listened to the sirens, breathed in and smelled the desperate, sweaty musk of his situation. He got up before the sun, just like back on the farm, and he rode the bus through black morning streets down to the docks and helped prepare a half-rotted fishing boat to launch out into the cold, wet mist.

One morning he counted the days since his last meal—a woman at his apartment complex had given them tamales, and they had eaten through them like locusts—and thought that after the tamales had been divided and devoured, the candy bar on Tuesday morning might have been his most recent food, three days ago. The cold crawled under his thin jacket like the fingers of death itself, and once when he stood up too fast on the boat, those black fingers covered his eyes for a moment and he steadied himself against the cabin. Later that morning he caught himself looking at the fish parts in the chum bucket, wondering what it would taste like, and that was the morning he called home.

He begged bits of money from his roommates, put his change of clothes into his duffel bag, and bought a Greyhound ticket headed north. He found a phone booth and called his dad to tell him but had to leave a message because, for some infuriating reason, the old man had never bought a cell phone. He said, "Dad, I've screwed up. I know I haven't met your expectations or God's and I have no illusions that I can walk back into the house and pretend everything's okay. I don't expect to be called your son. I don't expect you to talk to me or even acknowledge me. But I'm in a bad place and if you could even see fit to give me some work in the fields . . ."

Then his voice cracked and words failed him and he dropped the receiver back onto its cradle and he covered his face in his hands and pictured the clean rooms his father gave the hired men, with the single bed, the small side table, and the simple lamp, and Frank couldn't think of anything more beautiful and distant and impossible.

On the bus he rehearsed his apology over and over, his head against the dirty glass, the moon waxing above the horizon. Somewhere around Valencia the epiphany of how good he had it once upon a time hit him like a punch in the stomach. He prepared himself for his father's yelling, pictured the cords in his neck, his face flushed, the spittle flying from his mouth as he pointed at the land that had once been his. He took a deep breath and thought of his brother's self-satisfied grin. He considered the possibility that his father might not speak to him at all, that his father might turn him away at the front stoop, and that he would be really and truly broke and he wondered where he could walk from his father's ranch, where he could go if his father wouldn't hire him.

As the bus crested the Grapevine, he said a silent good-bye to Hollywood and Los Angeles and his so-called friends and felt himself and his dreams die and wondered why it had taken so long for the feeling of dying to come when he had stopped breathing years ago. He had taken Hamlet's dagger and used it on his father and himself and everyone within reach.

At Bakersfield the bus pulled in to take on new passengers, and Frank got off to stretch his legs. He took a short walk around the moonlit parking lot, trying to calm himself, trying to think of anything other than his destination and the comeuppance he knew waited for him there. Off in the corner of the lot he saw a familiar, beat-up green truck, alone in the pooled light of a streetlamp. He stood there, confused, because it looked like the worn, dented truck his old man drove through the fields. But of course that was impossible. The Greyhound wasn't even halfway to its destination. The dented green door opened and Frank's old man got out, covered in dust, still wearing his work clothes, as if he had come straight from the fields.

Frank dropped his head, and his hands fell to his side. He was sure the old man had come to tell him not to bother traveling all the way to the ranch, that there wasn't a place for him.

But his father raced toward him across the pavement and hit him like a train, his arms—strong as ever—locked around his shoulders and he said, "As soon as I got your message, Frank . . ." and he tried to say more, but the words caught in his throat, so he gestured to the truck, and the truck spoke for itself.

Frank got his duffel bag, and then they rode in astonished silence, Frank's eyes taking in the new geography as it sped past his window, moving him toward the strange familiarity of home. He felt regrets and years dropping away like miles. And then, when they got to the house, he shook his head and squeezed his eyes shut, trying to keep the tears in. Everyone in town had shown up. After all these years, they had all come to see him, the wanderer. There were steaks on the grill and music and lights blaring in the barn. He laughed in a stupor of wonder and hugged his father and danced into the barn. With a glad shout he joined the party.

When Jesus finished the original version of this story, he didn't comment on it. He didn't say anything about the angels rejoicing or heaven being glad when a son who has dishonored and shamed his father comes home. He didn't need to. I've talked to lots of people who have lost a child. It can happen so many ways: runaways or kidnappings or some unresolved fight or dying in a war or of cancer or a thousand other things. But one thing is always true: parents never forget their lost children. Never. The pain might mellow over the years. Maybe. But they never forget. They always want them to come home.

Jesus said that God looks at the lost like his estranged, runaway children. He just wants them to come home. When

Jesus sees the lost, he doesn't see people without a road map. He sees people who are valuable to God. He sees people who are precious to him. He sees poor, lost children, and he desperately wants them to come home.

So there you have it. Jesus spends time with the lost because they are intensely valuable, precious, beloved. But he doesn't stop there. He's not quite done with the story.

The Lost Son

Joshua takes a sip of water. His throat is tired. No one says a word. The kid with the crumpled joint in his pocket is staring at the table, blinking too fast, and from what the teacher knows of the kid's dad, he's not surprised. He knows Frank's story strikes the kid as improbable, as a fairy tale. The "happily ever after" isn't an ending most people expect in their own families. The story isn't done, though, not the one he's telling, and not the one that any person in the room is living. The teacher is reminded of this by the man with the dour face, who looks not only skeptical but as if he would like to climb into the story and give Frank a thrashing. Joshua clears his throat and starts again.

> Frank's brother was still in the field, working. Humberto came running out to tell him that Frank was home, that they were celebrating, that he should come see his brother. But the brother clenched his fists and refused to move, trying to shut out the glorious fanfare of the riotous party in his barn.
>
> His father walked through the dark fields until he found his son. He begged him to come join the party. His son trembled and clenched his teeth until at last he snapped, "All these years I've worked without com-

plaining and I've never once disobeyed you and you've never given me so much as a frozen pizza for me and my friends. But then *he* comes—your son who blew all your money on whores and marijuana and booze—and you make him a steak dinner? You throw a fiesta for the whole town?"

He kicked at the dirt and threw a clod of it out into the field with a furious grunt. "Have you even *yelled* at him yet?"

Silence. His father let the cool moonlight wash over them. The calm persistence of the stars was as distant and spare and clean as the distance between fathers and sons.

The father put a hand on the dusty shoulder of his son, but the son shook it off, glaring out into the darkness. The old man didn't step back, wouldn't give him his space. His father took his hand as gently as he would hold an injured calf and he looked out at the barn and the fields and everything around them and said, "Son, all this is yours. Use it as you please."

He searched for the right words to say, and as the wheat bowed its head in the moonlight he said, "I want you to understand—your brother—we might as well have buried him in one of your fields and planted a headstone. We never heard from him, we never saw him, no letters, no phone calls, nothing. But it's like we dug up his grave tonight and it was empty. Then we saw him walking down the road toward us, whistling and alive."

The old man shook his head. "How can you not celebrate a thing like that? He was dust and bones, but now he's flesh and blood. He was lost to us, but we've brought him home."

The teacher says this last sentence with his eyes closed. He doesn't ask if they have any questions. Instead, he listens to the rustling of their clothes, the shifting of their weight, the sound of their hearts like rock hammers in a quarry, trying to beat out a rhythm of new life. He doesn't expect them to understand, and he doesn't expect them to agree. He doesn't expect them to cry out and hold each other like long-lost siblings should. He doesn't expect that. He murmurs a prayer under his breath, and so long as his eyes are closed, he sees the silver-headed wheat bowing down in the moonlight, the golden light spilling over them through the open doors, and a holy breeze carries distant music, filling the air with contagious joy.

The Filthy, Torn, Broken, Lost

I understand why that church, once upon a time, wanted my friend to clean up before she came to church. I get it. We want people to come to Jesus with all their problems already figured out. Oh, we pretend that's not true, but as a culture Christians often adopt the role of the elder son rather than the role of the lost or the shepherd or the father or the ranch hand.

We see the lost running down the road toward home and before they get close we start shouting at them, "Hey! Not you! You're a homosexual!" This is not an exaggeration. I've sat in conversations and heard people say those words: A gay person cannot become a Christian. They need to acknowledge that homosexuality is a sin before they can come to Jesus.

Really?

We need to acknowledge sin in our lives in order to come to Jesus. But what if, for instance, a gay person admitted that she was a liar? And she came to Jesus and said, "I'm a liar and I know that's wrong and I want your forgiveness and I want to follow you."

Would Jesus tell her to go deal with her sexuality before following him? That would be a different story, wouldn't it?

In that version of things, Frank calls home and his dad picks up the phone and says, "Son, I want you to go make back all the money you lost and then come on home and we'll figure something out."

In that story the older son refuses to come to the party and the father says, "You're right to stay out here moping. I mean, your brother was dead to us, but let's be honest, just because he's alive doesn't mean he's perfect. Let's cancel the party."

Did you notice that the father never lectures his son on the way home? He never points out all the screwed-up ways he's a failure. He's just too thankful that his child has finally come home. Who gets the lecture? The one who's standing in the field with the sign that says, "God Hates People Who Take Their Inheritance and Waste It on Whores."

Jesus said that he didn't come to condemn the world but to save it (John 3:17). He didn't have to condemn it because it was condemned already. I can honestly say that I haven't met a person yet who didn't already know they were lost, broken, and in need of help. How can we not see that? How can you possibly read a newspaper or watch a news feed and not know that we as a human race are in desperate need of help?

No. To those who ask him, "Why are you spending all this time hanging out with the wrong crowd?" Jesus says, "Because they are lost. They are valuable and precious, and God's mind turns to them over and over like a father who misses his children."

Our mission—the same as Christ's—is to go to the lost and say, "All is forgiven." All is forgiven—because they know they've done wrong. Too often the fact of their wrongdoings, their shame, their guilt is what's keeping them from picking up the phone to say they can't bear another day in the slums.

Then we come along. The big brother. The big sister. We put our arms around the filthy and broken and torn and we say, "All is forgiven. Dad loves you. He values you. You are precious to him. He wants you to come home. Please come home."

4

The Good Neighbor

As the crowds around the teacher grow, so do the number of questions, the number of questioners. Today, a seminary professor named Dr. Jon O'Malley waits among the crowd for his chance to ask the teacher a question, to test him, to make sure he is safe. This is, after all, the job of the seminary professor, the pastor, and the spiritual leader, to guard and protect those under their care. He has been sitting cross-legged on the floor in the cramped living room for some time. It's not that the living room is small. No, it could swallow Dr. O'Malley's entire apartment, and the carpet is lush and worth more than O'Malley's car.

The influential people in the city want the teacher in their homes, they want people to know they know him. But it's not just the rich. In fact, to Dr. O'Malley's left sits a notorious corporate embezzler. On his right, uncomfortably close, her bare knee pushed up against his pant leg, is a woman of dubious moral character. Each of them listens to reports from the teacher's people all over the state. His people share that they have seen miracles, that God's word has gone forth, that God has done amazing things. All of which is well and good, but Dr. O'Malley has not come to hear about the teacher's ministry. He has come to investigate the teacher's theology, specifically his soteriology, his beliefs about salvation.

The teacher bursts into a spontaneous prayer of thanksgiving, and out of reverence Dr. O'Malley waits thirty seconds before he clears his throat and asks, "Teacher, how does one receive eternal life?"

The teacher grins when he hears the question, obviously pleased. His eyes search the crowd until he finds O'Malley and gives him an encouraging nod. "What does the Bible say? What's your interpretation?"

Dr. O'Malley, of course, doesn't need to think for a moment, as this is a topic of his particular expertise. "First, you must love God with your entire being, your entire heart, your whole soul, every ounce of strength, and with all your mind."

The teacher nods, then raises his eyebrows, as if he's waiting for something more, as if he is testing O'Malley and not the other way around. More than a few theologians would stop there, of course. But the question on the table is how to receive eternal life, and love for God is not, as he sees it, sufficient.

The professor takes a breath and finishes. "Second, you must love your neighbor as much as you love yourself."

The teacher claps his hands in pleasure and says with clear sincerity, "Well said. Do that and you'll live."

Dr. O'Malley wrenches himself from the floor, as if to go, then pauses. "May I ask another question?"

The teacher spreads his hands, palms up, as if to say, Be my guest. After all, he hasn't answered a question yet, not really. The professor takes his glasses off and cleans the lenses on the corner of his shirt, settling them back on his face so he can see the man clearly. The first command is clear enough. Love God. But the second. How could one know he had succeeded in loving his neighbor? How could he look at his life and say, *I'm on track. I did it*? The mechanisms of salvation matter, the details matter. O'Malley points at the teacher, making it clear that he expects an answer this time, that he won't be answering it himself. "And who counts as my neighbor?"

The teacher, sitting on a leather ottoman, leans back and with one hand reaches up and twists a lock of his hair. No one else says a word, they let the teacher think. When he finally speaks, he leans forward, his elbows on his knees, and he starts his story.

On a lonely stretch of I-5, headed south, a God-fearing trucker named Steve Ellisen got yanked from his cab and struck repeatedly with a tire iron, kicked in the ribs, and punched in the face until he lost his will to fight, along with all his money, three teeth, and his rig.

The teacher pauses here, letting them see the scene. The well-maintained but lonely road, the rubber skins shed by the tires of semis, the weeds trying valiantly to crack the blacktop. The growing pool of blood.

The teacher continues . . .

He lay there on the shoulder of the highway, struggling to breathe and wondering if his arm was broken because he couldn't feel it. He could feel his face swelling up and the sharp pain of something sticking him in the side. He wondered if he should sit up so passersby might see him. He tried and discovered that he couldn't.

Pastor Michael Johnson, driving south on a family vacation, saw the bloodied wreck of a man from some ways back. An excellent pastor of a popular church, Pastor Mike had a successful building project under his belt (the pews were already full—they were moving to four services), multiple book deals, a heavily downloaded sermon series, and a wonderful family. CNN called him when they wanted a spiritual perspective on the day's news. Pastors called him for advice. Common people called him (or at least spoke to his secretary) about their daily lives and how to live them. He was the pastor every pastor secretly loved, guiltily hated, or longed to replace.

As Pastor Mike's Toyota hurtled closer to the broken man on the pavement, he quietly shifted into the fast lane and called his wife and kids' attention to the view on the left side of the van, a low valley of trees punctuated by rocks. One of his kids said, "I don't see anything, Dad," and Pastor Mike took a deep breath and let it out slowly. He needed to shield his family from seeing something like that, a man brutally beaten and left on the side of the road. His kids were young and his wife was sensitive. Two hours later, when the cell reception got better, he quietly excused himself at a gas station and called to leave an anonymous tip with 911. He worked it into a sermon a few weeks later, something about protecting your family from the horrors of the world.

A half hour behind Pastor Mike came Levi Sherwood, a recent seminary grad on his way to interview to be the pastor at a small church in northern California. Levi got his MDiv from a respected seminary and was well known among the professors for his careful attention to the Scriptures and his encyclopedic ability to trace the history of and commentaries on the holy laws of God. As he drove, he rehearsed his Statement of Faith, testing himself and making sure he got every beautiful doctrine of God precisely correct. He was running, predictably, twenty minutes late and between his nervous chanting of soteriology and angelology he glanced, again and again, at his dashboard clock.

Levi almost didn't see Steve's broken body, but a bird flew in front of his car and drew his eye to the shoulder of the road. He saw the man, collapsed on his side. He thought maybe the bloody pile of flesh and rags was a corpse, but as Levi's car got closer, the man attempted to roll over and Levi saw his hand flop helplessly to his side. Levi hit the brakes and slowed to a crawl. He inched closer and closer to the man, checking his rear-view mirror to make sure he wouldn't be rear-ended. But the road behind him remained empty and desolate.

Levi pulled to a stop about twenty yards from Steve. He leaned forward, his nose almost touching the windshield, trying to tell if the man was breathing. A sudden thought that this could be a trap, that the man could be waiting to rob him and steal his car, burst into Levi's mind. Or more likely, that whoever did this to that guy might still be nearby, waiting for another victim. Paralyzed with indecision, Levi put his hand on the door handle, pulling it partway toward himself. The digital clock on the dashboard clicked forward, bringing with it the realization that Levi would never make it to his meeting on time if he stopped now, even if this wasn't a trap, even if he didn't get robbed. His hand loosened on the door handle and his foot weighed down on the gas, pulled by the tyrannical gravity of his schedule. He did his best not to get a clear look at the man on the side of the road and did his best not to look in the rearview mirror as he rolled past.

As the miles dropped away, so did Levi's worries and concerns, and he began to wonder if that had been a body on the side of the road after all. Maybe it had been a garbage sack or a mannequin. He laughed at himself and his overactive imagination and went back to quizzing himself on his theology. By his calculations, if he kept his foot to the floor and didn't get distracted, he'd only be about twenty minutes late.

The teacher pauses again, stretches his neck, and looks around the room, making sure he still has everyone's attention, because he's getting to the crux of the story. He taps his fingers against his jeans, as if considering the story he's telling, as if he's about to share an unfortunate truth, something he's not sure he's comfortable with but that has to be said. He takes a breath and begins again.

Now it just so happened that there was another man headed south that day, another fifteen minutes behind Levi. He was a devout man, in his way, and worshiped just as his father and grandfather and great-grandfather had done. He drove a Mercedes Benz, cream colored with all-leather interior, which he had only recently bought, though his wife assured him that they couldn't afford it. His name was Mohammed al-Jazari, and he marveled at the smooth ride and luxurious comfort his car provided. He drove often enough for business, and he thought this one small luxury should be afforded him, though his wife thought the money would have been better spent on upgrading their kitchen.

Mohammed, too, noticed the crumpled form on the side of the road and a mounting sense of horror grew in his chest as he came closer. His throat closed up, his eyes unblinking to the point of watering, as it became more and more clear that it was a body lying there, unmoving. He drove past the body, though not far, and pulled over onto the shoulder, leaping out of the car before it had fully stopped. He ran back along the road, the bite of sharp gravel coming through his loafers, and fell to his knees beside the swollen, bruised face of the man. He held his ear near the bloodied mouth. He reached for the man's neck and felt the pulse, weak but steady. Without hesitation—for Mohammed had served briefly in the military of his home country—he checked for broken bones and major sites of blood loss. Some of the ribs were broken, without doubt, as well as the man's nose and possibly his jaw.

Mohammed untied his tie, then tore off his shirt and quickly ripped it into strips. He bound the man's worst wounds, then sprinted to his car, drove it closer, and pulled the back door open. Getting the man off the ground elicited unconscious groans, and Mohammed struggled to drag him into the car. Great swaths of blood colored his backseat. Mohammed scrunched his suit coat into a ball to serve as a pillow, doing his best to balance speed with care. Then he called 911 on his cell.

When the ambulance pulled up, he jumped out of his car, bare chested and bloody, his heart thumping in his chest as he helped them move the man from his Mercedes onto a stretcher and into the ambulance.

Forty minutes later, amid a blur of lights and sirens, they arrived at the hospital. The man had no health insurance, no identification, no wallet. They checked him in, of course, but when Mohammed spoke with the admissions nurse, she made it clear that without proof of insurance, and with the man being unconscious, Mohammed should expect the minimum of care for the stranger in room seven.

Without a second thought, Mohammed pulled out his wallet and gave her a Visa card. "When that one hits its ceiling," he said, "I have another."

She brought him some documents, and he assured
her he would be legally liable for any expense the unconscious man brought to the hospital. He needed, now, to
continue to his meetings, where no doubt his colleagues
would ask him about his bloodstained slacks and the
scrubs he wore instead of a shirt. Perhaps he should
arrive even later and stop to buy some new clothes.
Regardless, he told the nurse he would return in a few
days to check on the man, and in the meantime she was
to see he received the best possible care.

When he slid behind the wheel of his car, he could
still smell the unconscious man's blood in the backseat. He put his forehead against the steering wheel
and prayed that the man would be well. More than
anything, he wanted the man to be well.

The teacher sighs, exhausted, with a faraway look
in his eye, as if the story is true, as if he has seen this
happen before. He closes his eyes for a moment, and
it's as if his eyelids are straining to stay closed but he
opens them again, his eyes focused, and he looks to
Dr. O'Malley and asks, "Which of the men was the
trucker's neighbor?"

Dr. O'Malley cycles through the potential answers
in his mind. He is concerned, most of all, that this is a
story about salvation, an answer to that most important
of questions, "What must I do to receive eternal life?"

Can it be that a Muslim, with his incorrect theology
and his corrupted religious practices, could be held up as
an example, as a part of the answer? Could the teacher
be saying that a man like that is somehow closer to
eternal life than a respected pastor or a sharp seminary
student?

Dr. O'Malley clears his throat. The story does not
leave him many alternatives. He cleans his glasses again.

He can hear the question echoing in his head: *Which of the men was the trucker's neighbor?* He can't bring himself to say, "Mohammed," or "the Muslim." At last he says, "The one who showed the trucker mercy."

The teacher nods. "He has taught you a lesson. Go do as the Muslim has done."

Dr. O'Malley opens his mouth to ask another question, but he finds that it will not come out. He turns the story over in his mind.

What was the teacher saying?

What did he mean by this?

And before a question can crowd its way from his mind to the narrow exit of his mouth, another of the teacher's followers has pushed to the front of the crowd, asking another question, on another topic. Dr. O'Malley listens to the question, but it doesn't make it past his ears, can't make room for itself in the compact turmoil of his mind.

He searches for a way out of the cavernous house but he has no guide and he wanders, lost. At last someone opens a door for him and waves him through, and Dr. O'Malley walks slowly down the sidewalk to his car. The whole drive home he watches the shoulder of the road, searching for answers among the broken glass and discarded soda cans.

5

The Billionaire and the Teacher

Everyone was asking the same question: "Who is this man?" He shows up, seemingly out of nowhere, and he's not the person we remember. He grew up in church with our kids and now, all of a sudden, he's teaching things in a way no one has heard before. He's saying things that make us uncomfortable; he's doing miracles and causing a stir. The word is some people are giving up their jobs, leaving their families to follow the man around and listen to him teach. Who is this man? Where did he come from? Why would people give up their lives to follow him?

I've asked all the same questions. Why would I want to give up my life and all the things I enjoy doing to follow him? What's the benefit? Church is okay, but I'm not going to give up my lifestyle so that if I get sick some old lady might bring me a casserole. Is there really a benefit beyond that? Sure, people say that if I believe in Jesus, one day I'll get to live in Heaven. But in the meantime, I'm living here now and the argument "One day you'll regret it if you don't follow Jesus" isn't particularly compelling.

I grew up in church, and the way I understood following Jesus was this: Jesus walks up to someone and says, "Follow me," and their eyes glaze over and they say, "Yeah," and they ditch all their possessions and off they go.

He finds a man named Peter by the ocean, fishing, and Peter shrugs and follows.

He finds Matthew at some sort of tax stand (I know this isn't right but I picture one of those tax preparation booths at the grocery store), and Matthew turns off his computer and follows.

Jesus finds a short guy up in a tree and says, "Hey, come down from there and follow me after you make me some dinner." And the guy says okay.

And in return, all these people receive the mysterious title of "disciple."

When I hear the word *disciple*, there are two possible pictures that pop into my head. The first is largely based around vague childhood memories of the TV show *Kung Fu* with David Carradine. I see a bald kid in orange robes who extinguishes candles with the wind from his fists, catches flies with chopsticks, hears his grasshoppers in the long grass and the constant beating of his own heart, and can walk on flaming coals. He lives in the high mountains. There is a master who calls the disciple "grasshopper" and teaches him to do things. This "disciple" learns how to do things so that one day he can humiliate some students of his own, or maybe move to the Old West and beat up cowboys.

The second picture that pops into my head is that of the bumbling followers of Jesus. They're the dummies who never get it right, who open their mouths at the wrong moment, or keep them closed when they should speak up. They never understand the simplest stories, the same ones I've understood since I first saw them on a flannelgraph in Sunday school. They're always scratching their heads because they don't understand things, fighting with each other, cutting off people's ears with swords, and betraying Jesus to the bad guys. They're the exasperating simpletons who constantly leave Jesus shaking his head and pinching the bridge of his nose and saying, "You still don't get it? Really? I guess I'll have to say this more plainly."

That picture isn't correct, though. The disciples of Jesus (today or two thousand years ago) weren't orange-robed martial arts experts or adorable sitcom idiots. These people—the "disciples"—left everything behind to follow this man.

Imagine you're standing in line at a crowded fast-food restaurant. The harried staff take frantic orders from exhausted customers, who want complicated things like a Cheesy Burger, hold the cheese, and an extra super large diet cola with a side of fries. In the midst of this, some guy flings open the glass door and elbows his way to the front of the line, leans over the counter, and says to the kid in the paper hat behind the counter, "Follow me."

The kid in the paper hat wipes the sweat off his forehead with the back of his hand, looks out over the sea of customers, nods, and throws his paper hat on the counter. The invitation is repeated to the other employees, and one by one they walk away from their stations, as if in a trance, step around the counter, and walk out the door in step behind the strange man. Meanwhile a Cheesy Burger lets off black smoke from the grill, and a fryer alarm sounds over and over. Someone is at the drive-through, their voice echoing into the restaurant. "Hello? Hello? Is anyone there?"

Or imagine this. You're walking through the big city. The skyscrapers form a canyon, the people cut through it like a stream, and you're bobbing along in it, headed on your merry way when someone hisses to you from a dark alley. Your feet slow, almost against your will, and your head turns to look into the shadows where a silhouetted figure beckons you to come closer. You turn toward him, leaning forward, trying to hear his whispered message, and he says it again, "Pssst. Hey. Come follow me."

He's moving deeper down the alley, and you call out, "Why? Where are we going?"

"I'm going to teach you how to catch people."

Catch *people*? No way. You pick up the pace and try not to look back over your shoulder.

Frankly, these stories don't make sense. No one would ditch their job to follow a stranger off the street who hasn't explained his agenda. No one would follow a man down an alley just because he said, "Come here."

What did Jesus's disciples know that made them want to follow him? What insight did they have that made them willing to leave everything?

Well, for one thing, when Jesus walked into a room, he changed it. Everyone went home that night and told their families what they had seen. He was remarkable. Amazing. Extraordinary. Weird. But we don't think of Jesus that way, as someone who should change us. We're perfectly satisfied with being the same as everyone else. Our plan has always been to do well in school, get a job, make money, be successful, and make our parents proud.

We have these mild, pleasant feelings about Jesus, because we've become too familiar with him. He's become ordinary to us. We've heard the stories a hundred times and nothing surprises us. Nothing amazes us. And how do we react when we meet normal, everyday people? Mostly we don't react at all. If someone asks, "What is that guy like?" we shrug and say, "He seems nice."

But let's be honest, many of the stories about Jesus are flat-out weird. For instance, he stalks up a white sidewalk in the center of a golf-course-perfect lawn and pushes open the door to a tract house. Family members dressed in black are weeping and dabbing at red eyes, and when he sees the little girl laid out in her funeral dress, cold and waxy, he says, "You can stop crying, she's just taking a nap." Everyone laughs at him. They threaten to call the cops, but then he takes her stiff little hand and says, "Little girl, get up."

And she does. She sits right up and asks for a drink, because that's what kids do as soon as they wake up. They ask for things.

Now imagine you were at that house and saw him do this. That night you go home, and one of your loved ones asks, "How was your day?" Would you shrug and say, "Fine"? If they asked you about the teacher, would you shrug and say, "Oh, he seemed nice enough"? No, obviously not.

The rumors about this man, Joshua, start to spread. Every day someone else has a story, and these extraordinary stories are repeated, spread, passed on, texted, emailed, blogged about, and forwarded endlessly until it seems like everyone has a story, everyone has something to say. The gossip starts rising to the top of society, sneaking in through service elevators and maids' entrances and whispered conversations among the chauffeurs.

These rumors, they're causing problems. Changing well-established patterns, throwing people off their game. Richard discovers this when his employer summons him to the office. When his boss calls, Richard answers, no matter if he's in the bathroom or at a ball game or on jury duty. So now, twenty minutes later, Richard stands in the spacious office, hands behind his back, and listens.

He's a good man. That's what Richard thinks when he looks at his employer, Samuel Abrams III. Samuel is just twenty-six and heir to his father's billions. Samuel has a way of asking for things politely and expecting the answer will always be yes, and why wouldn't he? That's the answer he's always been given. Right now he's sitting on the inner window ledge of an enormous plate-glass window, one leg carelessly resting on the chair in front of him, his tie loose, his coat on his desk, and his dazzling smile following the arc of the sun. He's leaning against the window, the skyscrapers framing him like his own personal picket fence, and he's prattling on about some teacher who is making waves, big enough waves that rumors of the man have made it here, to the fifty-second floor.

Samuel is a good man, and not just because he's rich. Richard has never known him to cheat someone or to tell a lie. He's generous, and not only with his employees. He gave several hundred million dollars to charities in the last year. Richard remembers once, when Samuel was a child, when they were walking on the street (not something Samuel did often) and saw two men in a fist-fight. "Why would they do that?" Samuel had asked. He didn't understand people hurting one another. Richard tried to explain, because that's his job. Not to shelter Samuel but to help him, to anticipate his needs. Richard still remembers Samuel's wrinkled brow as he considered the fistfight.

"It's not enough," Samuel says at last, and this phrase is one that pulls Richard back into the conversation. It's what Samuel says when he is unhappy, when he is about to make a change. He said it last year when he increased all the pension plans for his retirees. He said it two years ago when he doubled his charitable giving and started the Abrams Foundation. He said it three years ago when his socialite girlfriend admitted that she loved him, at least partly, for his money and social standing.

Richard bows his head slightly. "What is not enough?"

"The donations. The business. The politics." He laughs and waves his hand. "The Bible study I run on Wednesday mornings before office hours."

He strokes his cheekbone with his thumb, a habit he took from his father. "This teacher comes on the scene and if the rumors are true, he has nothing. Nothing but knowledge! He knows things I've been working my whole life to understand." He raps his knuckles twice on the desk, the sign that he has made his mind up about something. "I want to meet him."

"Forgive me, Samuel, but who are we talking about again?" Richard's job is to arrange such things, and when one's employer is a billionaire, it happens easily enough. Movie stars, senators, congressmen, captains of industry, dignitaries—they line up when they hear Samuel's name. At least, after a little work from Richard, they do.

This conversation leads to Richard finding himself in a run-down slum in the northeast part of town. This teacher, Joshua, can be found in church occasionally, or so he's told, but is more often among his followers, who are distressingly common. One moderately wealthy acquaintance of Samuel's, a man named Larry, told Richard where to find the teacher today but urged him to be patient. "Wait a week," he had said. "He's

leading a Bible study here at my house, and I'll invite
Samuel."

But Samuel doesn't wait, not when he has his mind
on something.

The rumors about this teacher are hard to believe.
People say he teaches in a way that makes people want
to go to church just to hear it, that he reads and understands those ancient words and talks about them plainly
so that his listeners understand them. Others say he
tells baffling stories without a point or that he is harsh
with those who come to him with problems. Richard
has heard rumors that the man is a healer, the sort who
tells people in wheelchairs to stand up. An ambulance
chaser. And yet, that's who Samuel wants to see, and
it's Richard's job to set it up.

He finds the teacher, finally, in the courtyard of an
apartment building. A narrow hallway leads to the center of a cross-shaped open space with the teacher at the
center. The crowd makes it difficult to get through. Texts
are coming in from Samuel, demanding to know if he's
found the teacher yet, and Richard writes back, "Yes, yes,
I've found him but haven't made it past the gatekeepers
yet." The crowd is crushing in on the man. Richard can
see him up ahead, hundreds of people between them.
In fact, the only people who seem to have a chance at
getting to the man are children who are squirming and
wiggling and crawling their way through the rabble. One
of the teacher's people shoos them off, but the teacher
laughs and draws them close and is saying something
about it. Richard is too far away to hear.

Thirty minutes later Richard, with the judicious use
of elbows and shoving and at least one bribe, has made
it halfway to the teacher. A small commotion breaks out

behind him. He looks back to see a limousine on the street and Samuel standing on the sidewalk, adjusting his cuff links. Those in the back of the crowd are sizing him up, wondering if Samuel might be able to fill their needs as well as this unreachable teacher.

The crowd doesn't part for Samuel, not exactly, but with his bodyguards as blockers and his impressive presence, it takes him less than three minutes to make it to Richard. Samuel has clearly tried to dress down for the occasion—he's wearing his Dolce and Gabbana black pinstripe suit, one of his common suits he wears to soup kitchens and low-end benefit dinners, but in the sea of denim and polyester, he stands out like a pearl among marbles.

Richard and Samuel stand there for five minutes, straining to hear the teacher's words, until one of the teacher's followers notices the rich young man among the peasants and plunges into the crowd, pulling them up toward the teacher, who is sitting on a white plastic pool chair. He's young, younger than Richard at least, and his skin and hair are dark, his face weathered, his hands large and calloused. He wears work boots and jeans and a cotton T-shirt, his hair long and not well brushed. The teacher's people pull up another chair for Samuel, who smiles his thanks and sits. Quick introductions are made, but never one for small talk, Samuel says, "Good teacher, what must I do to inherit immortality?"

The question surprises Richard. First, Samuel has never used the term before, never given any indication that living forever is something he's concerned with. It makes perfect sense, it's just not something that Richard had considered. Second, Samuel's terminology: What must he do to "inherit" a never-ending life. Of course that's how he thinks. Everything he has was inherited from his father.

Joshua smiles, creasing the wrinkles by his dark eyes. "Why do you call me good?" He waits, watching Samuel, waiting for an answer.

Samuel is clearly taken aback. He meant the honorific, no doubt, as a sign of respect, but the teacher is seemingly taking him to task over it. Samuel is not used to this sort of treatment, this borderline disrespect.

The teacher leans forward, as if confiding a secret. "There's no such thing as a good person, except for God. Only God."

There's a twinkle in his eyes, as if he's asking Samuel to deny this, to argue, to fight him on this statement. As if he's asking Samuel, "Are you saying that I'm God?" But that can't be, of course not. Who would ever make such a claim?

The teacher stands and now, when he speaks, his voice echoes over the crowd, loud enough for the others to hear. He is teaching the crowd now, not just answering Samuel's question. "You know what the Bible says. Don't cheat on your spouse. Don't murder, don't steal, don't lie. Treat your parents with proper respect."

Joshua looks back to Samuel, who nods, clears his throat, and says, almost embarrassed, "Ever since I was old enough to know better, I've lived by those rules and never broken them."

It's true. Richard has known him forever and he can't think of a time when Samuel knowingly broke these rules.

Richard stands near enough to see both of their faces—Samuel, with his look of humble embarrassment, and the teacher, who gazes back at Samuel with undisguised delight.

Samuel has always despised braggarts, and now with clear eyes he looks to the teacher, seeking his approval. The teacher crouches down beside the plastic chair and his large hands clamp onto Samuel's biceps, wrinkling the sleeves of his suit. His smile is warm with affection and he says, "You're only missing one thing. Go sell your possessions and give all the proceeds to those who have nothing. Then come join me."

Samuel crumples in slow motion, like a paper tower in the rain. Then, slowly, he stands, the teacher's hands still on him. With careful, deliberate steps he makes his way back toward the edges of the crowd, his bodyguards flanking him. This time the crowd does part, and the teacher watches him go, every step, and stands silent while the chauffer opens Samuel's door. The black car pulls away from the curb and disappears down the street.

The teacher turns back to his people, his voice soaked in sadness, and says, "It's so hard for wealthy people to enter God's kingdom." He shakes his head and takes his seat. "Harder than driving a semi truck through a keyhole."

There is a gasp from the crowd. A dread settles in Richard's chest and, deeper than that, an angry denial. Samuel is a good man, despite what the teacher says. He's the sort of man that people around the world desire to be. He's devout and kind and cares about those around him. Richard clenches his fists and blurts out what he can only imagine others are thinking, "If *he's* not good enough, how can the rest of us possibly get in?"

"It's not possible," the teacher says, his eyes seeking Richard's.

The crowd reels, as if they had received a blow, but he doesn't stop there. "Human beings can't do it, no matter how hard they try." There's that hint again of merry laughter in his eyes. "But God can do things that human beings cannot."

A man with giant arms and a great black beard says, "We've abandoned everything to follow you."

The teacher places a reassuring hand on his arm. "Make no mistake. If you've left behind your home or your wife, your brothers or sisters or parents or children because of God's kingdom, that sacrifice will be paid back with interest—high interest, and in this life. And in the age to come, you'll live forever."

And there it is in a moment. The so-called secret of the teacher, revealed moments after Richard's boss got in his limo and rode, sad-eyed, back to his office. Richard sees two paths stretching out before him. He can continue to serve Samuel's family, trying to be like them: wealthy, kind, powerful people who constantly think, *This is not enough.* Or he can throw in his lot with this strange collection of children and blue-collar workers, homeless people and cripples. All of them have given up what little they had in the hope of finding immortality, hoping to become like this man, hoping to be near him. It's more than that, though, isn't it? Richard sees a disturbing subtext to the words. It's as if the teacher is saying . . . but that can't be. It's as if he's saying that one's entrance into God's presence isn't dependent solely on being a good person but rather on one's proximity to this teacher.

The teacher glances up and notices Richard. He doesn't move but his eyes lock on Richard's and he says, simply, "Follow me." Then he stands and steps into the crowd.

Joshua is moving now, the crowd gliding around him like smoke around a campfire. Where is he going?

Richard's phone buzzes. It's Samuel. He wants Richard on the fifty-second floor right away. Richard stares at the tiny letters on the screen, and in his peripheral vision the teacher is getting away from him. He wants to see more. The man puzzles him, and he wants to hear him teach, wants to see if these supposed healings are real or just ecstatic rumors. He turns his phone on silent and slips it into his pocket. The teacher turns down the street, and Richard follows.

6

Only Everything

It's a mystery to us when someone like Richard or Peter or Matthew gives up his livelihood to follow Jesus. I have a lot of questions about this concept, but there are two questions I really want answered: What did those early followers think it meant to "become a disciple of Jesus"? And what did they honestly know about Jesus that made the sacrifices to follow him worthwhile?

In first-century Israel, there was a special meaning to the word *disciple*. The word *disciple* (*mathetes* in Greek) could just as easily be translated as "learner" or "student."

Jesus invites people to become learners, students. For many of us, the word *student* gives us flashbacks to high school or college, when we walked into math class with one objective: to walk out understanding decimal places and denominators and dividends. We wanted to gain the knowledge and insight of our teacher. But the first-century concept of discipleship had a lot more to it. It lacked the emphasis on the impartation of knowledge. It's not that the impartation of knowledge was unimportant in discipleship. For instance, when Jesus's disciples come to him and say, "Lord, teach us to pray," he answers with specific directions about prayer (Luke 11:1–13). But the central concern of student and teacher was something more than the student gaining knowledge.

Look at what Jesus says about the role of student and teacher, disciple and master: "The student is not above the teacher, but everyone who is fully trained will be like their teacher" (Luke 6:40).

He doesn't say, "A student who is fully trained will know what their teacher knows." No, he says that the student will *be like* the teacher. A disciple adopts the teacher's lifestyle to become like the teacher. What if, instead of just learning algebra from your math teacher, you adopted your math teacher's lifestyle? What if you ate the same food, lived in the same house, wore the same clothes, graded the same papers, studied the same brainteasers, made the same complaints in the teachers' lounge? A disciple is not being given their teacher's knowledge. A disciple is learning how to live like their teacher.

The decision to follow Jesus hinges on one question: Do I want a life like his? Or, if you prefer, do I want to be a human being like Jesus? As you can imagine, this alters the parameters of decision making. That kid in the fast-food restaurant isn't just thinking, *What can I learn from this guy?* but rather, *Can I become like him if I ditch my job and follow?*

Do I want that? Do I want to be like Jesus? The responses of people to Jesus in the Scriptures are described using words like *worship*, *astonishment*, *marvel*, *amazement*, *terror*, *fury*, *awe*, *repentance*. This is the sort of thing the rich young man in Luke 18:18–30 would have heard before he met Jesus, and he certainly would have understood Jesus's instructions to him as an invitation to become his student, his disciple. If Samuel wanted to adopt Jesus's lifestyle, he would have needed to make some changes.

Someone like Samuel comes to Jesus with what we think should be an easy question: "What must I do to inherit eternal life?" Jesus's answer, eventually, is, "Give up everything and come follow me."

We spend a lot of time talking about the cost of following Jesus. If I choose to follow him, what will I have to give up? What might he ask me to do? Where might he instruct me to go? What might he tell me to say? These are important questions. Jesus said that before someone builds a skyscraper, they should sit down and do the math and make sure they have enough money to buy the materials and pay for the contracts and get the permits. Otherwise they might get only halfway done and have to abandon the project. Then the skeletal remains of the unfinished building will be a constant reminder that they couldn't do what they set out to do, and people will mock the builder. So it's not that we shouldn't talk about the cost of following Jesus. Jesus talks about it himself. He says, "The cost of following me is only everything."

Doing the Math

The deal is a bargain. You want to live forever? You want to have a life like Jesus's life? Good. You should want those things. You can't buy them. You can't work hard enough to accomplish them. It's not possible for human beings to do that. But it's possible for God, and he says, "I'll give this invaluable prize to you in exchange for whatever you have." Joshua had a story about that, too.

Roland is walking around at the flea market. It's an open-air space, and every once in a while between the stalls of homemade driftwood clocks and antique store leftovers and worthless comic books from the 1990s, he finds something interesting, something valuable. A Beatles 45, maybe, in near-mint condition, still in its sleeve. Or an original, handmade Alfred Shaheen Aloha shirt. A piece of scrimshaw on mammoth bone. The sorts of things that can be bought and resold at a profit. Roland doesn't have tons of cash but he has enough to scrape out a living this way.

Then one day he discovers something amazing. He's halfheartedly flipping through some old movie posters shrink-wrapped against cardboard backings and there, between a *Casablanca* reproduction poster and a beat-up Jimi Hendrix concert poster, is a bundle of original art. He picks it up and pulls it out and looks at it closer and his heart starts pounding.

The first page is a man in tights, wearing a cape and holding an automobile over his head. He's smashing the car into the ground while men in suits scurry out of the way. With shaking hands Roland continues to flip through the bundle and finds eight glorious pages of inked comic book art. He sees the signature in the corner of one page and he cannot believe it. Jerry Siegel, one of the creators of Superman and the artist who invented the iconic hero.

Now Roland knows that a "very fine" copy of Action #1, the first appearance of Superman, sold for a million dollars at auction. Because it's so old, finding a copy with clean white paper and tight edges and a crisp spine is rare. But this appears to be the original art for Action Comics #1. And it's signed by the artist, the cocreator of Superman. He realizes that these eight pages could mean a new life for him. Each page could bring in a couple million dollars and the cover, well, he could probably set any price he wanted for that and it would sell. These eight pages literally mean the difference between shopping at the flea market and shopping on Rodeo Drive.

Does the owner of the stall know how much the pages are worth? Probably not. Not if he's bringing them here to the flea market and wedging them in with the posters. Roland tucks the pages under his arm, picks up the *Casablanca* poster, and gets ready to haggle. "How much for these posters?" he asks.

The owner grins at him, a sparkle in his eye. "A hundred bucks for the Bogart poster. And four hundred grand for the Superman pages. And that price is firm. No haggling."

Four hundred grand! The pages are worth way more than that, at least ten times that. Probably more. Roland starts doing the math. His house is worth maybe half that. He could sell his car. All his flea market finds would have to go, and his watch. In fact, he would probably have to sell his clothes, his skis, his television, his computer. Maybe, just maybe, if he sells every last thing he owns, if he maxes out his cards and gets a loan and gets a fair price on the house, he might be able to scrape up the four hundred g's.

So he shakes hands with the man and says it's a deal and races home to sell his house and his car and his clothes and his computer and his kitchen pans and his hammock and his cuff links and his waffle iron. And it's not much later that, penniless and homeless, he walks away from the flea market with some priceless original art tucked under his arm. He's wearing his oldest pair of jeans, torn and paint-spattered, and a pair of flip-flops no one would buy. He doesn't even have enough change for bus fare.

But with each step toward the auction house, his smile grows brighter.

The True Cost

We spend a lot of time focused on the cost. We ask questions about whether we'll be happy if following Jesus means giving up certain things: that new sports car, the multilevel mansion, the intense hatred for that coworker, the ability to ignore the dirty, homeless man on the corner or the mass graves being dug in some remote despotic empire. We imagine someone like Roland, standing there with his mouth open, arguing with the owner of the Superman pages. We imagine him deciding, *You know, it's not worth it*, and sliding the art back between the movie posters.

But Roland doesn't leave the flea market dejected. He doesn't leave scowling or dwelling on his sacrifice. He leaves whistling. He can't wait to brag to his friends about the amazing deal he just got. He'll do a showing where he frames each page and lines a wall in a gallery and by then he'll be a millionaire and his friends will say, "How much did it cost?" and he'll say, "It was a bargain. It only cost me everything."

We spend so much time focused on the question, What will it cost me to follow Jesus? that we forget another, equally important question: What is the cost of not following Jesus?

I saw an interview once with a famous actress. What she said boiled down essentially to this: "I know this will sound ungrateful. I've been called the greatest actress of my generation. I've been paid generously for my work. I have a great boyfriend and I'm famous and sometimes I find myself driving the streets of Los Angeles and crying because it's not satisfying. You think being rich will satisfy you, but it doesn't. You think being famous will satisfy you, but it won't. There has to be something more than this."

What is the cost of not following Jesus? It's an unfulfilled life. It's continuing in spiritual poverty. It's living with personal brokenness. The cost of not following Jesus is remaining with the status quo.

The cost of following Jesus is only everything. You can't follow him unless you're willing to become like him, and if you want to be like him, you can't remain like yourself. We can't say to him, "I want to be like you, but please don't take away my broken places."

The cost of not following is brokenness.

The cost of following is transformation.

Worth It?

When Peter and Matthew and that guy in the tree and hundreds of others made a decision to follow Jesus, he had not yet mentioned eternal life to them. They weren't signing up to go to heaven when they died. They didn't even know he was God, didn't know he was the savior of the world. He had not yet promised them anything more than a life like his life. And they said, "Yes, I want that, and it's worth everything I have to go after it."

Many of us know so much more about Jesus than Peter did or Matthew or any of those earlier followers. So why are we still wrestling with giving him everything? Why is it so hard? Could it be that we don't know him as well as they did? Or could it be that, like Samuel, we are focused on the cost of following instead of the cost of not following?

To become his disciple means not primarily to *believe* in him but to *become like* him. As we get to know him, we have to ask, *Would I be willing to follow a person like this? Do I want to be like him?* He's inviting us into his work, his mission. Is it worth "only everything" to follow him?

If so, we should hang out with the type of people he hangs out with. We should share his message, do the miraculous.

We need not only to believe the right things but to act on them. We should focus on becoming like him.

When Samuel gets back from meeting the teacher, he looks over his empire. Billions of dollars. Homes all over the world. Private jets. Vacations with influential people. Anyone just a phone call away. A kitchen staff that creates banquets at his whim. A personal assistant who anticipates his moods and needs. A yacht, designer clothes, and classic cars, and an aching certainty that somehow *this is not enough*.

He plays with the numbers, wonders what it would look like if he started dropping zeroes from his net worth. He sends an email to his financial manager, tells him they need to talk first thing tomorrow, that he needs some advice. He wonders if he really wants to be like the teacher if it means giving all this up. He wonders if a camel can really thread the eye of a needle. He wonders if a semi can fit through a keyhole.

7

Playing Simon Says

Ever since Jessica was a little girl, she knew she didn't want to be like her mother. She never knew her dad. Mom worked hard as a waitress, barely scraping together enough money for them to live on. Jessica loved her, of course she did, but she saw the dark circles under her mom's eyes and the sad way she opened up another can of tuna and left it on the counter for Jess's dinner, and Jess thought, *That's not for me. I'm going to live a better life. I'll never leave my kid home alone to eat from a can while I'm off at work.*

The symbol of the better life for Jessica was this magazine advertisement that her mother had ripped out and put on the bathroom mirror. It was for a perfume, a really expensive perfume called Baccarat. It was French, and her mom told her once that it cost thousands of dollars an ounce. An ounce! For her mother, it was a picture into another life, and it comforted her to know that somehow, someway, that could be out there for her. Maybe if she hadn't had Jessica so young . . .

And Jessica decided early on, she couldn't remember exactly when, that she was going to be the sort of woman who had a bottle of Baccarat on her shelf, who dabbed herself with luxury before going out with her high-society friends.

She didn't have any illusions about what this would take, and she got a job early and she worked hard and she got into a good school. The trick with school, of course, was that she was burning through money, sinking deeper in debt and it was an accident, really, when she found out that she could make money dancing.

She was at this bar with her friends, and there was this amateur dance competition. The girl who won did so because she had been sexier than the other girls and had excited the men in the crowd. So a week later, Jessica came back, entered, and won $150. Just like that, in a mere thirty minutes of work.

She didn't like to dwell on what happened in the years after that. Honestly, it had happened so slowly and so unexpectedly that she barely understood it herself, but she had taken a job dancing at this club and the money was pretty good, but it was better if she was willing to take more off, better still if she was willing to get close to the men in the audience. When she started giving the massages, she started making some real cash. And one day, she realized the money could be even better with a little more work, with one more little sacrifice. And it had been pretty easy, actually, to take that last little step over the line.

So she had money coming in and way faster than when she was working as a waitress. She wouldn't say it was easy money, but it was money all the same. Was she happy? No. She felt horrible half the time and angry at herself for feeling horrible the other half. She had money to burn and moved to New Orleans for a while, thinking she could get better pay there, but she got pregnant. She had to get an abortion and that set her back for a while, so she came back home and set up again in the old place.

She bought some Baccarat when she had the discretionary cash to do so. Saved and scrimped for it, and put it on the table in front of her mirror. She wore it on her dates sometimes, because it made her feel worth something, made her feel like this is what she had planned all along, to be this woman, to get paid to go on dates. That's how she thought of it.

Then One Day

One day she heard about this guy, this preacher who was coming through town. Some people Jess knew had hung out with him at a crazy party and said he was amazing. Really amazing. They claimed he said things no one else had ever said. Her friends said that he treated people like her, people like them, with respect. She laughed when they said that, the idea that a preacher could look at her and see anything other than a sermon in the making. She didn't believe her friends, not for a second. But she heard that he was going to be at this rich guy's house, a rich church guy, a real stuck-up jerk named Simon. She'd seen him around, knew where he lived. And there was this thing in the paper saying it was an open house. Everyone was welcome.

Jessica tried to put this all out of her mind, but it kept bothering her. And that night, when she was sitting in front of her mirror getting ready, she noticed the dark circles under her eyes and thought how much she looked like her mother. That decided it. She put on her best clothes and, almost as an afterthought, grabbed the Baccarat and threw it in her purse.

She parked her beat-up old Buick at the front gate of Simon's house. For some reason she was embarrassed to drive up in it, so she walked up the long driveway to the giant front doors. She was wearing her long leather coat, her favorite red shirt, the tight, sleeveless one, and she had on a short skirt and tall, heeled boots. As soon as the woman in the evening gown opened the door, Jessica knew she looked like a tramp. She looked cheap. And everyone in the party would think so. She could see it in the woman's eyes.

She walked through the giant atrium, past the chandelier, past the marbled stairway, and into the dining room. Many of the guests, obviously rich, were sitting there in their tuxedoes and evening gowns, and she thought maybe she'd made a mistake, maybe this was a wedding reception or something, but then she saw him. The preacher.

He was still wearing his coat, just like her. No one had offered to take it at the door. He was wearing a pair of beat-up jeans and a T-shirt, and she could tell, she just knew, why the rich people had invited him. They wanted to see him like you want to see the circus. A novelty. An interesting evening's entertainment.

And she couldn't stand it. She clenched her fists and felt something bubbling up inside her chest. Those jerks were looking at the preacher the same way the men looked at her in the club. They wanted him to dance for them. They wanted him to give them something to talk about, some exciting little diversion. They welcomed him like you welcome a clown to a birthday party. He wasn't a guest, he was the main event.

She went straight to him, trying not to grind her teeth, and asked if she could take his coat. There was a startled moment of silence at the table—she had interrupted their conversation—but he said yes, and she took it and went to the hallway, found the closet, and hung it up. Then she came back and saw that his water glass was empty, and she filled it, and she didn't know what she could do for him, but his eyes looked tired, too.

If there was one thing she knew how to do well, it was giving someone a massage. So she put her hands on his neck and she started to work on his tense muscles. He didn't turn. He didn't say anything. And as she worked the kinks out of the cords in his neck, as she strained her fingers trying to relax the muscles in his shoulders, she felt tears squeezing out of her eyes, running down her face. Giving this preacher a massage wasn't enough.

She thought of the perfume in her purse and how it made her feel special, made her feel worth something, and she took it out and she shook some into her hand and rubbed it gently on his neck. She splashed more on her hands and rubbed them over his neck, but the perfume didn't come out fast enough and finally she put it on the table and smashed the bottle open and soaked up the perfume in her palms and brushed it into his hair and rubbed it on his cheeks, and she was weeping and she started to kiss him over and over and she couldn't stop kissing his cheeks and his neck and his hair and he still didn't say anything. He didn't tell her to stop. He didn't flinch. He didn't pull away.

She noticed Simon's face. Anyone at the table would know what he was thinking. *If this man was really a preacher, if he was really a prophet from God, he would know that he shouldn't let this woman near him.*

And the preacher said, "Simon, I have something to tell you."

Simon said, "What is it?"

"There were two people who had borrowed money from someone. One of them had borrowed $35,000 and the other $350. Neither of them had the money to pay the lender back. So he decided to forgive them both their debts. Who do you think will love the lender the most?"

Simon straightened his bow tie and replied, "I suppose the one who owed the most money."

"That's right," the preacher said. And then, for the first time, he turned and looked at Jessica, as if he had just noticed her. "Do you see this woman?"

Of course he had seen her. They had all seen her. Everyone here had known the moment Jessica came in. How could they have missed a woman from the wrong side of the tracks, who doesn't even know the right clothes to wear to a party? She had massaged the teacher in front of them, broken a bottle of perfume on the dinner table. What a ridiculous question, "Do you see this woman?"

The preacher cleared his throat. "I came into your house, Simon, and you didn't take my coat. She not only took my coat, she massaged my shoulders. You didn't so much as shake hands with me, and she can't stop kissing me. You didn't show me where I could wash my hands, and she has covered me with expensive perfume. She's done a lot of things wrong in her life—her sins are many—but she's been forgiven. You can tell, because of how much she loves me. Because if someone has been forgiven a small amount, they only love a small amount."

Then the preacher turned and looked right at her, so she could see his eyes, and he didn't look away. He put his rough hand on her cheek and he said, "Your debts are all paid. Your sins are forgiven."

And the table started buzzing with conversation. Who was this man to say that he could forgive sins? Only God forgives sins. The preacher smiled at her and said, "Your faith has saved you. When you leave here, leave at peace with yourself and with God."

Jessica walked out of that mansion and down the driveway and back to her beat-up old Buick. And do you know what was funny? In all the years to come, despite all the things that happened to her, despite all the stupid things she did, those few sentences meant more to her than any bottle of perfume.

"Your debts are all paid. Your sins are forgiven."

She wrote his words on a little square of yellow paper and she put it on her mirror and never, never took it down.

Scandal

This story is inspired by Luke 7:36–50. A religious leader named Simon invites people over to his home to meet Jesus and hear his teaching, and then this sinful woman comes into Simon's house, weeping. She kisses Jesus's feet until they're wet with her tears. Then she lets down her hair and starts to wipe his feet clean. She kisses his travel-worn feet and pours perfume on them.

I can imagine all the religious people whispering to one another. *Scandal.* They're too polite to say anything, but Simon pops his monocle out and stares across that table full of filet mignon and caviar and he can't believe what's happening.

The scandal wasn't that this woman had come into a rich man's house. In Jesus's time it was common for people to host teachers in their homes and hold an open house for the neighborhood. She wouldn't have been turned away at the door. It's like if you were holding a Bible study at your house and your neighbor knocked and asked if she could come learn about the Bible. Of course you would let her in, because you're a good person, a religious person. And it would probably be good for your corrupt neighbor to hear what this teacher had to say.

So the scandal wasn't that the woman came into the house but that she came close to the teacher. She could listen to him without causing a stir. She could learn from him without raising too many eyebrows. But to think that she could walk up to him, to think that she could touch him! That was not appropriate. She was a sinner, and whatever sins belonged to this woman, they were public enough that everyone in town knew about them.

And I hate to say it, but in that culture, at that time, a woman taking her hair down for any reason was unquestionably sexual. Completely inappropriate. And she was touching him and kissing him. Many commentators think that the woman in this story was a sex worker of some sort, probably a prostitute. It's likely that the perfume she used on Jesus's feet was one of the tools of her trade.

Simon thinks, *If Jesus were really a man of God, he wouldn't allow that woman to touch him,* and I would have thought the same thing. If some traveling Christian speaker came to your town, someone you weren't sure of, and you opened up your house to him for dinner, and a prostitute walked into the house, sat down on the couch next to him, and started combing her fingers through his hair, wouldn't that make you nervous?

You might ask yourself, *Is it really wise for this pastor to allow her to touch him that way? Does he know she's a prostitute? Does he know that verse about avoiding the appearance of evil?*

And Simon thinks, *If Jesus was a prophet he would know that this woman is a sinner.* Because if he did know who she was, he wouldn't allow her so close. He wouldn't let her take down that long, meticulously brushed hair, and rub it over his feet. He wouldn't let her moan and cry and kiss his feet practically without coming up for air. If we asked Simon why he thought like this, I'm sure he would say the same thing we would. Sinners should not be that close to godly people.

That woman was a sinner. No question.

A Sinner at the Dinner Party

The woman might have been a prostitute. We don't know, because the Bible doesn't say. But we do know that she lived a sinful life, and that it was obvious to everyone around her. Her "sins are many." Simon looked at her and judged her and knew she wasn't good enough. And then he turned to Jesus and started to judge him too. That's what's happening when he thinks, *If Jesus was a prophet* . . . If Jesus was a godly man. If Jesus represented God. If Jesus knew what was happening. If he was good enough. If he was more like Simon, if he knew what Simon knew . . . If Jesus knew all these things, and if he was a prophet, he would never allow this woman to put her hands all over him. Simon kept circling back to the woman, to this important point. The woman was a sinner.

Which brings us to this question: Wasn't Simon a sinner too? Apparently not. He didn't look at himself and think, *What am I doing, sitting at this table with the man of God? If Jesus really knew me he'd know that he should keep his distance.* No. Simon didn't see himself that way. But we know the truth. The Bible says, "All have sinned and fall short of the glory of God," and "There is no one righteous, not even one" (Rom. 3:23, 10), and maybe Simon would have signed off on that idea. But he just wasn't that bad. He had it together. He was a religious guy.

Jesus saw all this in a moment and he told Simon the story of two men in debt. I don't know if you've been in debt, but I have, and it's not a good feeling. You're constantly looking at your account balance and thinking, *How can I possibly get out of this hole?* You're wondering how you can make ends meet, how you can possibly squeeze another dollar out of your life or spend one dollar less. Many times in history being in debt meant you could be thrown in jail if you failed to pay. There wasn't bankruptcy protection.

One of the two men in this story owes a month and a half's salary. Not a small chunk of change. The other owes a *year and a half's* salary. That's sizeable! Both are in debt, though, and neither has the power to come up with the money he owes. Neither one has another dollar to give the lender.

So he forgives them. He gifts them the money and says, "You never have to pay this back." Jesus asked Simon which of the debtors would love the generous lender the most, and he grudgingly admits that it would probably be the one who owed the most.

Then, in this weird moment, Jesus turned to the woman weeping at his feet and asked if anyone had noticed her, which of course they all had. He said this:

Do you see this woman? I came into your house. You did not give me any water for my feet, but she wet my feet with her tears and wiped them with her hair. You did not give me a kiss, but this woman, from the time I entered, has not stopped kissing my feet. You did not put oil on my head, but she has poured perfume on my feet. Therefore, I tell you, her many sins have been forgiven—as her great love has shown. But whoever has been forgiven little loves little. (Luke 7:44–47)

The things Jesus mentioned—water for his feet, a kiss of greeting, oil for his head—weren't necessarily expected in that culture. It wasn't necessarily rude to fail to wash a guest's feet or to neglect to give them oil for their head. Jesus had been treated within the realm of good manners. On the other hand, no one had gone out of their way to make him feel like an honored guest. If someone important had come to Simon's house—let's say the governor—he would have certainly enjoyed these amenities and probably more.

Simon or Jessica?

If you're like me when you read this story, the sinful woman is the good guy, Jesus is Jesus, and Simon is the dumb slob. As soon as I read the story that way, though, I'm taking the role of Simon. I'm judging him for his sin, laughing at him for his spiritual inadequacies. Oops.

The fact is, I'm like Simon. I'm always "bringing my best to Jesus." We like that, bringing all our wonderful attributes, all our great sacrifices, all our amazing service and laying it all at the feet of Jesus. We wear our fancy clothes to church, we "do our best," we try to make ourselves look good, like we're doing something special.

I do this all the time. Look at me! I write books about God and spiritual things, as a service to him. This is a wonderful thing.

But I forget that God wrote the bestselling book of all time.

Look at me! I'm a good speaker and I love to travel and tell people about Jesus and teach them from the Word of God. I love to get up front and sacrifice time with my family so I can serve him in this way, through my speeches, through the spoken word.

But I forget that when God spoke, he brought the universe into being.

I can brag about my academics and say, "I worked hard at school and this 4.0 is a gift to Jesus." God didn't even go to school and he knows literally everything. He has a four-billion-point GPA.

Do we understand this?

Take some enormous human achievement, like the Sistine Chapel. Michelangelo spent years on his back, painting his masterwork, a painting that is universally acknowledged as one of the great artistic works of the human race. Perhaps Michelangelo will stand before God and humbly say, "God, I'm bringing you my best, look at this amazing piece of art."

But God made the entire universe: quarks and black holes and human beings and the duck-billed platypus and cumulonimbus clouds and gravity and lava. Michelangelo painted angels and clouds and the human anatomy, but God created all the things that Michelangelo copied and arranged on that chapel ceiling. Michelangelo holds his arms out, showing God the Sistine Chapel, and God kindly accepts it. I'm sure it will be on God's refrigerator when we get to Heaven.

Our greatest accomplishments are nothing compared to what God can do. And while I absolutely love it when my kids bring me a piece of artwork from preschool, I don't stick that piece of paper with the cotton glued onto it ("Those are sheep, Daddy") on the fridge because it's a stunning piece of artwork. I do it because that horribly proportioned, teacher-assisted, sticky mess of a picture shows that my kid loves me and wants my approval.

Everything we bring to God, every sacrifice, every piece of praise, it's trash. It's garbage. It's nothing compared to what he himself could do. He's glad to accept those things, he wants them from us, but when we get to the place where we think we're doing him a favor, we've lost sight of reality. We're Simon, thinking how lucky Jesus is to come over for dinner.

We need to stop playing the part of Simon, sitting at the table and ignoring our sin. Jessica always gets closer to Jesus than Simon, because she's not trying to prove that she's worthy. She already knows that she isn't. She's not trying to hide or deny her sin, she's not trying to pretend that her life is all together and perfect.

We don't hide our brokenness. No, on the contrary, we bring our broken places like broken pieces of a perfume vial, and we lay them at his feet, weeping. And he says, "What you have brought me, this is beautiful in my eyes."

We bring him our brokenness. We tell him, "Hey, I'm a liar, a cheater, a thief. I'm proud. I'm selfish." We bring him the hundreds, the thousands of sins in our lives because our sins are many. And if we hide our broken places, how can he possibly start the process of repairing us? We bring him this perfume, not because it's "the best" but because it's the best thing we have. How did we get it? Where did it come from? Well, where did the woman in Luke get the perfume? How do you think she paid for it? What sinful acts produced it?

We bring our broken places to him, our garbage, our perfume, and we come scandalously close. Then God turns and he looks us right in the eyes and he says, "*Your debts are forgiven.*"

We stammer an objection in the midst of the objections of every person at the table. Can that be true? Can he really forgive me? Does he understand, really, the horrible things I have done?

But he does. He does understand how deeply broken we are. He does understand the consequences of that brokenness. He understands it more than we ever will. And he says, "*Your debts are forgiven.*" It's time to let them go. It's time to stop living like someone with a debt to repay.

Am I Simon or Jessica? Either way, I've been forgiven. Simon looks at his life and thinks, *Oh, that wasn't such a big deal. I'm a good person.* He doesn't see much reason to be thankful. Jessica knows how much she's been forgiven, and Jesus says you can tell that she has *already been forgiven* because of her great love for him.

If I'm Jessica and I know already how badly I need a way out, how much I crave forgiveness, how unworthy all my offerings are, then I take those things to Jesus and accept his gracious forgiveness.

If I'm Simon, then I'm unaware of how much I should be thankful for. I'm not aware that all my offerings can come only from my own brokennes, until he makes me whole. He delights in repairing me, in using my fallen places as opportunities to increase my service to him. After all, his power is made perfect in our weakness.

8

Mister Miracle

The news hits Drew in the gut. His teacher is dead. Not just dead, but humiliated, dragged from his cell and killed, execution style, in front of a drunken and drug-fueled party, complete with feasting and strobe lights and dancing.

They dragged him out of his cell and a guard put his pistol at the base of his skull, and when it was done, people applauded, if you can believe that. He was a good teacher, a great man, despite his strange habits, living as a homeless man outside of town, eating insects and whatever he could find, never taking a handout, never accepting money from his followers. He didn't drink, didn't brush his hair, wore homemade rags, and yet Drew is not afraid to say that he loved him. He remembers how he told people to share their wealth with the less fortunate, how he told the government fee collectors to stop gouging people, how he told the cops to stop extorting people and to never accuse someone falsely. And he remembers the day that his teacher told him it was time to leave, pointing to another man walking by.

"Look! The sacrifice who will take away all the guilt of the world!"

So Drew followed Joshua without question. He knew he was the one who had been predicted by God's spokespeople for generations. He witnessed the blind being able to see, the deaf hear, the lame walk, and with sincere purpose he brought others along to see the new teacher, including his brother Pete, strangers, whoever crossed his path.

But now to hear that his old teacher is dead, it's not what he expected at all, and he's starting to wonder, maybe this whole thing isn't going to play out the way he expected, with Joshua ascending to power and overthrowing the corrupted government. On top of that, they barely have time to eat, let alone to mourn, because any house or building Joshua enters is immediately flooded with the stinking, squalling mobs of broken, sick, twisted humanity. And yet the teacher won't quit. He keeps teaching, keeps welcoming in more sick to pray over, even lets the children sit on his lap. He doesn't stop and that means his followers can't stop either.

So it's with some relief that Drew hears the teacher say, "Let's get out of here for a while."

He tells Pete and Drew to get their boat ready. It's a commercial rig and they haven't taken it out in a while, but it still smells of diesel and fish guts and there's a familiar ritual as they prepare the trawler.

Drew says, "Batten down the hatches, boys," in the pirate voice their father always used, and they both laugh. Pete gets some food ready and there's a cooler sitting on the dock and before long the teacher shows up, dark circles under his eyes and a small smile on his face, and the other ten climb aboard, and the boat is full but she's strong enough, and they make way for a place they know across the sound.

The teacher settles in on the bow, watching the waves as they plow through them, the spray and the sun uniting in a glowing nimbus around him, while Bart pulls out the sports equipment he brought. A baseball game is in order, he says, and Pete says there's an old stadium not far from where they're headed. James and John start arguing over who will get to bat first, and Jude says he's a great switch hitter, and soon it's all baseball and sunshine and waves. The teacher is napping for once instead of teaching or praying or healing people, and for a minute Drew forgets about his old teacher, the murdered one, and enjoys the bickering and jokes and the smell of the water. Pete decides to drift for a while and fish with his rod instead of the nets, and for once, a fight doesn't break out. Drew drops down into a warm, contented sleep, with sunshine as a blanket.

An hour or two later the engine rumbles back to life, and Pete heads toward shore. He hasn't caught any fish, of course, but that wasn't the point. Drew closes his eyes, his fingers folded over his stomach, until Pete shouts to him, and before he even opens his eyes to look, he can hear them.

They're crowded onto the dock, shoving and pushing and desperate and they barely move when Drew yells at them to get back so he can tie off.

A sea of expectant faces look up to the deck, surrounded by wheelchairs, hospital beds, and makeshift gurneys. Joshua returns their gaze, his face drawn in a look of deep sorrow. He tells his followers to start moving people toward the baseball stadium. Bart sighs and throws his baseball glove over his shoulder, and soon they're bumping wheelchairs across the grass. Pete has pulled the chain off the fence, and people are filing up into the bleachers. This place used to be a minor league ball stadium and it's a good thing because there's got to be five thousand or more people.

The teacher stands near home plate and starts to teach. He's telling them all how happy they are, how blessed, to be who they are. It's a message his groupies have heard before, how even the poor or the mourning are better off than the rich and the privileged. They're all glad to hear a message like this, sure, but the fact is that a lot of them have come because their legs or eyes or ears or hearts don't work and when he puts his hands on their heads and turns his face toward heaven, God shines down on the man. There's a steadily growing collection of useless wheelchairs near the dugout.

Drew is on crowd control. He's walking up and down the bleachers, asking people why they've come, trying to help the sick ones down the stairs. There's a crazy guy shouting at everyone in the tenth row, and Drew moves him to the front of the line before he hurts someone. There's a kid on crutches, a woman hacking up a lung, a guy with blood oozing down his forehead and getting in his eyes. There are others who've come for the spectacle or because they want to hear the teacher's lessons. There are skeptics and fools, preachers and con men, pimps and housewives, lawyers and anarchists.

As the day wears on, the sun turns the stadium into a convection oven, and people are moving into the tiny patches of shade, following them around the bleachers.

As the hours pass, the number of sick people shrinks, but the crowd has only grown. Night is coming, and people are hungry. Some of them have traveled a long way and are weak with hunger. So Drew grabs Phil and they pull the teacher aside. Joshua's other followers see something is going on, so they all come down from the bleachers and soon all thirteen of them are standing at the pitcher's mound in a knot. The teacher's voice had been getting hoarse, so they give him a drink. He asks what they need. He's always asking people this. "What is it that you want?" That question, it's his weakness; and whatever your need, he fills it.

"The people are hungry and it's late," Drew says. "They haven't eaten and it's a long drive from here to anywhere. Let's dismiss them so they can get something to eat."

The teacher nods, as if he agrees with Drew, as if he sees the point. Then he smiles and says, "Don't send them away. *You* feed them."

They're standing there on the pitcher's mound and they all turn at once and look at the crowd and then back to the teacher in the center of their huddle. Phil says, "To give everyone a light snack would cost twenty-five grand. Is it really worth it to spend so much for so little?"

The teacher doesn't say anything. Pete realizes he forgot the cooler and it's sitting on the dock on the other side of the sound. Drew snaps his fingers. "I just remembered. I saw a kid with two hot dogs and five buns earlier in my section."

Several of the guys mutter things at him. Thom asks if they were kosher dogs, and James makes a joke about how there are always more buns than hot dogs. Drew wishes that James could control his tongue for once but he realizes that's a lot to ask.

The teacher says, "How much food do you have? Go check it out."

Drew runs up the stairs and finds the kid, explains that he needs the food. The boy doesn't make a fuss, doesn't object, just hands his plastic grocery sack over. People are milling around, restless now that the teacher isn't speaking. Drew runs up to the teacher and holds the bag open for him to see. "What good is this for so many people?" he asks.

The teacher takes the bag and looks inside. "Tell the people to sit down," he says, "in groups of fifty."

Then he walks to home plate and holds his hands up and tells everyone to sit. Once everyone is seated, he calls his followers back to him, and Drew and all of them gather around.

The teacher takes out the bag of hot dog buns and pulls the five buns from the plastic. He holds them over his head and he looks up toward the sky, the stars washed out by the lights of the ball field, and he gives thanks for the bread. Then he starts pulling the buns apart and handing them to Drew and the other followers. And he keeps handing them more bread, and more, and more. He breaks the bread and he hands it over, and he goes down the line, handing more buns to each of the men, and they start to take them up into the bleachers.

Drew has his arms full of bread. The people in the crowd don't seem to think much of it at first, but when he finds the kid who sacrificed his lunch, he hands him five buns and says, "Eat all you like." The kid is amazed. Ripples of whispers are moving through the crowd. Drew doesn't ration, doesn't stop anyone from taking as many as they like. And then he goes to get some hot dogs and there are thousands of them, stacked in rows, waiting for him to deliver them. He personally hands out at least five hundred.

Finally, he has a moment to eat one himself. The teacher is sitting on the pitcher's mound, his legs crossed, his jacket folded across his jeans. He smiles at Drew and Phil, and they crouch down beside him. They don't understand how he did it. Some of the others are still walking up and down the aisles, so Drew takes another armful of food up the stairs. The people in the crowd wave him off. They're stuffed.

The teacher tells them not to waste the food, a command that surprises Drew, because if he can do this sort of miracle, why would he ever be worried about wasting food again? He can always make more. But they find a box of clean garbage bags, the big ones. They climb into the bleachers, waving their bags, and everyone passes in the food they can't finish. Drew watches in wonder as the bag fills to quarter full, then half, then overflowing. He's dragging the bag down toward the diamond, trying not to lose any of the food teetering at the top, his arms aching.

He's almost to the bottom when a large man with tattoos on his giant arms pulls him over and says, "He's the one, isn't he? The one who's going to fix everything."

Drew doesn't know what to say to that. A second voice calls out, "If he can do this, if he can feed us all, that's more than the current government is able to do. We should put *him* in as our leader!"

There is cheering. People start talking about weapons and the quickest way to make Joshua their ruler. Drew tries to calm them, but this isn't a conversation about staying calm, and he's ignored. Eventually he leaves them and pulls his trash bag over to the teacher, amazed by how much food there is, how much more than what they started with, and he looks up and sees that the others are coming with their bags, and their bags are full too. There are twelve waist-high garbage bags, all of them filled with bread and meat. It's overwhelming. It's amazing. Drew doesn't understand how it happened. It doesn't make any sense.

The teacher says, "You twelve go ahead and get the boat ready and head for home. I'll catch up with you after I dismiss the crowd."

They do what he tells them to do. From the boat, Drew can see the lights in the stadium. He thinks about John, his old teacher, the one who was murdered, and he thinks how much John would have loved to have seen this. Drew shakes his head. It's not possible. The healings, those aren't possible either, but Drew has grown accustomed to the "everyday" miracles. This one was different. He can hear the crowd. They're chanting the teacher's name. He hears the teacher's voice rising up in the midst of their chants. He imagines him on home plate, palms up, asking them to stop their cheering and chanting.

After the boat is ready and the running lights are on, they pull out into the sound, and he can still hear the noise of the crowd. Cars are starting now, wending their way back toward home. Drew sits heavily in the stern of the boat, his hands trembling. *These hands. These hands held two servings of food, literally a handful of food. And now thousands of people have eaten from it.* He tries to stop his hands from shaking but he keeps thinking, *I did that. I was part of that, somehow.*

He looks up at the stars, bright and blazing against the black sky. Is there anything the teacher can't do? He remembers the teacher's words when that rich young man came to him: *It's not possible. But God can do things that humans cannot.*

He shudders and rubs his arms with his hands. He closes his eyes and listens to the engines and the slap of the black waves against the hull. What does this mean? He doesn't know. But one thing is certain. He will never tell the teacher, "This is not enough," again. He can't wait to get to the other side and see him. He can't wait to hear the next lesson. Who knows what tomorrow might hold?

Waiting for a Miracle

Sometimes I catch myself waiting for a miracle. I see a need or a problem and I think, *Why doesn't God step in and take care of it?* That's pretty much where it ends for me—a little complaint, a small nagging thought that God ought to clean it up, because he has the power and I don't.

What fascinates me about Jesus feeding the five thousand is that his followers are the ones to suggest that the crowd needs food. Actually, in one account, Jesus suggests to Phillip that he should take care of it ("to test him" because Jesus had already decided to feed them all himself), but that harmonizes easily with the other accounts. Basically the disciples look at the world around them and they see people in need, so they approach Jesus and say, "Hey, we should let these people go get something to eat. They're going to stay here forever so long as you keep teaching. Give them a break and let them go."

When I first noticed this, it took me by surprise. It seems to me that Jesus came from Heaven with an agenda, and part of that agenda was doing miracles to prove that he was someone different, someone who should be listened to, that he is and was and will be God. But in this story he's responding to someone else's agenda, someone else's observations. His followers are the ones to say, "There are some hungry people here. Let's get them some food."

It's important that we not run away from this. Jesus does this miracle because something is requested of him. If you take a few days and read through all the stories about Jesus, you'll notice something. The vast majority of the miracles follow this pattern: someone asks Jesus for help, and Jesus provides it.

In case you're skeptical about this, consider these other miracle stories.

> Mary, Jesus's mom, comes to him at a wedding to inform him that they've run out of wine. So Jesus turns water into wine. This is his first miracle, and he does it because his mother asks him to save the party.
>
> Blind people call out to him, "Jesus, have mercy on us!" When he asks what they want, they say, "We want to see." So Jesus heals them.
>
> Peter asks Jesus to help his mother-in-law, who is sick in bed.
>
> People come to him and say, "My servant is sick."
>
> A group of friends break in through a skylight and lower their crippled friend into the room where Jesus teaches.
>
> A sick woman presses her way through the crowd to touch the edge of his jacket, hoping for a reprieve from her sickness.

Jesus doesn't "volunteer" a miracle in any of these situations, and in fact the woman in the crowd "forces" a miracle. Most often someone asks for a miracle. Jesus is responding to the requests of those around him.

This is not to say that Jesus is our lapdog and will do whatever we request. He's not beholden to us. If we pray on our way to a crowded mall at Christmastime, it doesn't automatically mean we're about to see the Miracle of the Front-Row Parking Space. There were times during Jesus's ministry when people requested a sign or miracle and they were turned down—Herod, a government official, for instance (Luke 23:8), or the religious authorities (Matt. 12:38). Their requests seemed to be more along the line of "Prove yourself to us" or "Do something neat," and Jesus barely took the time to answer them.

To be clear, I'm not suggesting that if someone comes to Jesus today and asks for a miracle and doesn't receive it, this means they are lacking in faith or asking with wrong motives. God can and does allow us to have illness or difficulties in life that are not signs of our own sin or issues but that God permits for his own reasons. Notice, for instance, that the great missionary and teacher Paul said he was given a "thorn in the flesh" that tormented him. Whatever that was, he asked God to remove it three times, and God refused. Paul's conclusion was that it had been given to him to help keep him humble and he goes on to say that he had also been weak and persecuted and lived through hardship and insults (2 Cor. 12:6–10). I defy anyone to say that this is because Paul didn't ask God for help or because he didn't have enough faith.

The point, however, is that we're not sitting around waiting for Jesus to do a miracle. *He's waiting for us to ask for one.* This observation created a radical shift in my own life. When I see someone in pain or when I'm in pain myself, I know that I shouldn't sit back and hope God does something about it. I have to go to him and say, "Lord, this person is in pain. What can be done about that?"

And then I wait, breathless, for his reply.

9

A Ghost on the Sea

Let's give them a free dinner. You guys take care of it."
Jesus had seen the crowd, like lost kids at the zoo with
no one looking for them, and felt sorry for them. He
sat them down and started to teach. He prayed for the sick
and they were well. He filled the empty with the fullness of
his words. And as the heat of the day beat down on them in
that remote place, as the crowd got ready for the long journey home, through the dark, their stomachs rumbling from
a day without food, something happened. Jesus's followers
had a moment when they saw the crowd the way Jesus did.
They saw them standing there outside the penguin enclosure,
small and alone and hungry, without so much as a sack lunch.

And they said, "Jesus. Let the crowd go so they don't faint
on the way home. They're hungry."

When Jesus responded, it wasn't with heavenly bread falling out of the sky. Instead, he listened carefully to their request
and answered in a way that seemed both impractical and
shocking. "You feed them."

It's the same with our requests for intervention. Jesus listens with, I suspect, interest and compassion. Then, invariably, he responds to our demands by telling us, "You do it."

Honestly, it's amazing to feed five thousand people with one sack lunch (not hot dogs, of course, but fish and bread), but would it have been any less amazing if it had been five hundred people?

Once I was part of a team of twelve missionaries in a city of six million people. This was in a country where the government was hostile toward Christianity and many of our daily activities were illegal. If caught, we could have been deported. Government officials had tapped our phone lines and broken into our apartment to go through our papers.

There were only a handful of Christians in the city, and we wanted every person in that city to know about the Jesus who lives and breathes in the real world. We used to laugh and say, "There are twelve of us and six million people. If we each tell half a million people about Jesus, we can go back home."

In the face of a situation like this, when the sheer impossibility of a task threatens to drown us, it's natural to say to ourselves, *I'm inadequate for this.* And that's good. That's exactly what we should say. We are inadequate to accomplish the impossible. We have insufficient power to do the miraculous. Jesus's followers said this exact thing when he suggested they feed the hungry mob. Philip said two hundred silver coins wouldn't be enough to give everyone even a mouthful of food. Two hundred silver coins (the specific coin was called a denarius) would have been about eight months' salary.

But Jesus said, "You don't have enough to feed these people. Go figure out how much you do have." What his followers brought him was woefully inadequate. But he nodded and said, "That's enough." It's enough because he never expects us to accomplish the impossible without him. He merely wants our participation.

He could have made lunch for all five thousand people with a clap of his hands. He could have brought down manna from heaven. Instead, he took a little boy's lunch, brought to him by his compassionate followers, and handed it back to them to serve to the crowd, allowing them to participate in the miracle. Jesus gave thanks and gave the bread to his followers.

Who fed the five thousand? His followers did. They're the ones who walked among the groups of fifty, all seated on the grass, and brought them their dinner.

We ask for the miraculous, and he expects us to participate in the miracle he provides. We are inadequate and we realize we don't have enough. He tells us to simply bring everything we do have. We bring it all, even though it's insufficient, and he makes up the difference using his divine power.

So when Jesus agrees to fix the wedding party after his mother asks that of him, he requests that the servants bring him water. He tells a man with a twisted hand to stretch it out. He tells a man with withered legs to stand up and walk. At the very least, he asks us to participate in his miracles by having faith. He doesn't need our faith to do the miraculous, yet he often tells people in Scripture, "Your faith has healed you." We provide faith or water or fish, and he provides the miracle.

Who Is This?

In the darkness on the water, Pete and Drew wrangle the boat toward the far shore. A vicious wind has risen, howling across the deck. Their friends are wedged into corners and have fought for the dry spots or covered themselves with tarps. The waves slam into the hull, and the boys, exhausted and soaked in their yellow rain slickers, coax the boat forward. Drew wipes the sopping hair out of his eyes and looks at his watch. Four in the morning.

Pete yells something, but his words whip away toward the stadium. He's waving and pointing starboard. Drew grabs hold of the railing and looks out over the monster waves. There's a white shape, tall and thin, moving through the wind, leaning forward, not bobbing like a buoy but standing on the water like a man on uncertain, rolling ground. Drew throws his hood back, straining to get a better look. Whatever it is, it appears to be passing them.

Pete comes to his side and Drew barely spares him a glance. The wind whips the water against his face, stinging his cheeks. "What is that?" Pete shakes his head. He doesn't know either. The others start to line up, shouting against the wind. Drew doesn't know who says it first, but someone almost whispers, "It's a ghost."

A chill runs down Drew's spine and jumps like an electric arc from man to man down the line. What else could it be? A shape that walks like a man, that floats along the water, that stays on top of it as if the water has skin. The men start to panic, shouts and cries rising from their throats in a primal, terrified chorus.

Then a voice pierces the wind. "It's me! Don't be afraid."

The shouts stop. They know the voice. It's the teacher. They look at each other nervously as the ghostly shape rises up on a wind-powered wave and then slowly drops down again. Pete shouts something that doesn't make any sense at all, his voice hoarse and nervous. "Sir, if it's really you, order me to walk out to you."

For a moment, they hear only the wind, and then the teacher's voice says, "Come on out."

Pete, with barely a hesitation, throws off his slicker and jumps up on the rail. Drew thinks to reach out and stop him, but Pete has already jumped feet first into the water. Or rather, onto the water. He lands with a thump, his knees bending against the water below him. He stumbles toward the shape on the waves. Everyone is shouting, advice, fear, wonder, and disbelief spilling from the boat and into the air.

Like a newborn horse, Pete moves on shaky legs toward the teacher, who is walking toward them across the water. The wind hasn't stopped, though, and the waves are large. Pete almost trips when a wave picks him up. He steals a look back toward the boat and then at the water and waves threatening to dunk him. When Pete looks back, Drew sees a look on his face that he's seen rarely but knows all too well. He saw it on Pete's wedding day. Saw it once when one of their crew was knocked overboard as they passed a pile of fish that had frenzied sharks gorging on the edges. He saw it when they were children and a mugger had threatened their father. Pete is bone-shakingly terrified. And just like that, he starts to sink. Slowly at first, up to his knees, and then he drops like a man falling through water, which is precisely what he is. He barely has time to shout, "Sir, help!" Then Drew sees only Pete's hand, reaching up out of the water. Drew pushes James aside and grabs a flotation device.

The teacher runs toward the spot where Pete sank, his hand outstretched. There's no sign of Pete now, and the teacher stands over the spot and reaches down into the water, like a man reaching into a sack, and he yanks

Pete out by the collar. They can hear Pete coughing and sputtering, every sound brought to them by the wind, and then the teacher's voice, "You have so little faith. Why didn't you trust me?"

He throws Pete over his shoulders in a fireman's carry. He walks up through the wind and rain, and the men lean down to take Pete from him and pull him back into the boat. The teacher grabs two of the twenty hands reaching for him, and they yank him aboard. He helps move Pete to a sitting position, and when he straightens up, the wind stops and the water is calm and clear. The stars shine down on them, and they can see the lights onshore dead ahead.

Drew finds himself on his knees and he realizes the others are in the same position. They're clumped around the teacher, and he's looking down at them, his hair soaked and plastered to his head.

Drew says, almost whispering, "It's true. You really are God's son."

Then they're all talking, shouting, babbling about him, about how amazing he is, and Drew realizes that if he had been paying attention, if he had understood what was happening when Joshua fed the five thousand, he wouldn't have been surprised when the teacher walked to them on the water. *He can do whatever he wants. Just because something is impossible for a human being doesn't mean it's impossible for God.* All of Drew's questions about the teacher and who he is drain away. He can do things that only God should be able to do. Who else could he be?

From that day forward, everywhere they go, people start to line the streets with the sick. It's like a parade: wheelchairs and hospital beds and feverish, weak people clutching tissues, all waiting for the teacher to pass by. They shout to him, asking for permission to touch the edge of his sleeve so they can be healed. They keep asking him for a miracle, and when they reach out their hands and touch him, he provides one. And Drew knows—everyone who was on the boat knows, even if they don't say it—this is not just another pastor, another preacher, another prophet. It's true. He's God and he does what he pleases.

The Only Thing We Bring

More often than not, Jesus does the miraculous in response to a request for help. He expects our participation, however, and sometimes asks us to bring everything we have to the table, even if that's not enough to make up even 1 percent of what's needed. Notice that in the account of Peter walking on water the same thing happens: Peter asks Jesus to command him to come out on the water, and Jesus does. Despite the fact that he is a professional fisherman, Peter has absolutely no ability to walk on water. All that he's bringing to the miracle is his request for a miracle and the faith required to obey Jesus, following his commands.

When Jesus fishes Peter out of the water, he doesn't say, "Well done, Peter. You're only the second person in the history of humanity to walk on water. You're the best." Rather, he says, "You of little faith. Why did you doubt?" God expects the impossible of us, and he's disappointed when we say we believe he can accomplish the miraculous but instead allow our doubts to prevent us from participating in that miracle. When we fail to have faith, we're revealing the limits of what we think Jesus is capable of accomplishing.

This is a moment when Jesus is proving to those around him that he's more than a man. He's God. What is impossible for humanity is possible for him. The Mark account of Jesus walking on the water says that, after Jesus climbed into the boat, his followers "were completely amazed." And why were they amazed? "For they had not understood about the loaves" (Mark 6:51–52). In other words, if they had really connected what was happening when Jesus handed out that bread, they wouldn't have been surprised to see him strolling along through the hills and troughs of the rough sea. God does what he likes.

So God does not ask us to accomplish something without empowering us to meet the demands of the task. There are times when we see a need in the world and ask God to do something about it . . .

Lord, why are there so many orphans in the world?

Why are there cities where people do not know the name of Jesus?

Why are people of a certain ethnic background mistreated in my community?

In response, God commands us to act to alleviate the need we have seen. He gives us an impossible task.

Do we jump into the work, keeping our focus on the man who stands on the waves? Or do we focus on the wind whipping around us? If I catch myself saying that I don't have enough time or money or experience or ability or strength or resources or people to accomplish this thing in front of me, then I need to stop for a minute. That's like Andrew saying, "We don't have enough food to feed all these people," or Peter saying, "I can't walk on water myself." Of course you don't. Of course you can't. We're inadequate to do the miraculous.

When we say, "I can't do this miraculous thing being asked of me," what we're really saying is, "I don't believe God can do it."

And so here we stand in the presence of God, wearing a wet rain slicker, with a sack lunch of bread and fish. We can't feed a crowd with what we have. We can't walk on water. But that's never been the question. The question is, Do we believe Jesus can do those things? And, if so, do we want to ask him to intercede?

10

The Savior Who Doesn't Save

Martha understood what it was like, spending time with the miracle worker, the teacher. He could be infuriating. Cryptic. Obscure. Then he would wave an ambulance down and pull a crash victim, broken and hemorrhaging, from the back. He would lean down and whisper encouraging words to the swollen face of the victim and undo the straps holding the man to the gurney and say, "Get up!" and the man would. He would swing his feet over the edge and stand up, and the paramedics couldn't believe it, and there the man would stand, whole but wearing shredded clothes, whooping and singing and suddenly jumping and dancing in the street, washed red and white in the lights of the ambulance.

Once Joshua came to their house to lead a men's Bible study. Her brother Larry had invited him, had hosted him, and the men packed out the house. She had spent the whole morning cleaning, buying groceries, getting ready. After the men arrived, her sister, Mary, kept pausing at the doorway to the living room, a platter of canapés in her hand, still and silent as a cat. Martha moved her along, but ten minutes later Mary was standing in the back of the room, unobtrusive. Martha grabbed her by the arm to get her help setting the table. The next time Mary managed to sit on the arm of an easy chair and then finally she wedged herself in among the men, sitting by the teacher's feet, her arms circling her knees and her eyes wide with adoration.

Martha tried to do the preparations herself. She did, for she had a gift for hospitality, but between rotating things in and out of the oven, getting pitchers of drink ready, and arranging flowers for the table, she nearly burned the bread. She marched into the living room and squeezed her way in toward Mary, whispering at her to come and help. The teacher looked at her and smiled, and Martha, mortified, realized he had stopped teaching to see what was going on.

"I'm trying to get everything ready and I can't do it myself. Would you please, please tell Mary to help me get the food ready?"

She would never forget his words or the deep affection in his voice when he said, "Martha, you're so worried about everything! Relax. There's only one thing that matters. You've chosen to fix dinner and clean the house." He nodded toward Mary. "And Mary has chosen to do something better. No one is going to take that away from her."

To say she was shocked was an understatement. She muddled through somehow and got the meal ready. She realized that on some level she wanted to sit in that room too. She wanted to crash the men's Bible study.

And the teacher, he didn't care at all that Mary wasn't moving food into the oven, filling pitchers, or arranging the flowers.

The next morning, after everyone had gone, Larry stood in the kitchen, washing the dishes with Martha. As she rinsed them and handed them over, Larry rubbed them dry and put them away and tried to explain everything the teacher had said, his stories, his insights, how he answered questions with authority. Mary wandered in and sheepishly helped with the cleanup.

In the days that followed, the teacher ate with them often, stayed at their house sometimes, dropped by with his followers. Over time a deep bond formed. He loved them, and they loved him. Mary got almost giddy whenever she heard he was coming to visit. Larry would clear his schedule. All three of them wandered out into the city sometimes to watch him teach and pray over people. Larry donated money to his band of followers, handing over thick wads of cash to Jude, who worked as a sort of de facto financial officer for the group. He gave often, as much as he was able, as well as dinners and use of the house on top of that.

So when Larry got sick, Martha didn't worry. The teacher said she worried about so many things, but not this one. After all, she had seen Joshua touch a man's clouded eyes and watched the glaucoma disappear. She had been twenty feet away from a woman who had been bleeding continuously for decades and was healed when she touched the teacher's jacket. So a little flu, a little fever didn't bother her at all.

Larry's condition quickly worsened. He lost his strength, couldn't even sit up to sip water, and Martha and Mary took turns sitting with him, washing his brow with a cold washcloth. Martha sent the teacher a text message that said simply, "Larry—your beloved friend—is sick."

He didn't text back.

She might have understood that. If he had been on his way, too busy to write back, she could have understood. If he had dropped everything and run to them, if he had called to say why he couldn't come, if he had sent a messenger, if he had done any of those things, she would have understood, at least she thought she would have.

But he didn't do any of those things.

Soon the doctors suggested taking Larry to the hospital. They said he would die either way. There was nothing to be done. Larry refused to go. He would rather die here, in his home, with his sisters. He didn't want the beeping machines, the constant invasion of the nurses, the fluorescent lights. They spent the last hours together, Martha by his bed and Mary sitting by the open window, watching the long driveway that led to their house and saying over and over, like a mantra, "He'll come. He'll come, Larry, you'll see. Hang on."

They thought that Joshua loved them. He said that he did. He acted like he did. But if he loved them, even if he only loved Larry, wouldn't he be here by now? They thought he was powerful, they knew he was, they had seen it with their own eyes, but if he was so powerful, why didn't he do something?

Larry still talked to them sometimes, but with his eyes closed and from somewhere far away. He was getting pale and his skin was papery and dry as a lizard's. Then he took that breath, a deep, shuddering breath, and when he breathed out it was more than air, it was everything, everything that made him Larry. Martha shouted for Mary, who stumbled to the bedside, and they held his hands as his fingers got cold and then stiff and they washed his face with their tears and held each other. She hadn't held Mary in a long time and she was glad to know that at least her sister was warm and breathing and alive. Her poor sister shook with sobs, and Martha was sobbing too but still she could just make out the words that came in gasps between Mary's wails, "Where was he? Where was he?"

Martha rubbed her back and tried to speak, her voice cracking when she said, "I don't know, honey. I don't know."

He's Here

Now Joshua is on his way, or so Martha has heard. He didn't come when Larry was sick. He didn't even show for the funeral. It has been three days since they buried him and now Joshua shows? Now she gets a text from Pete, telling her they're at a rest stop outside of town?

She doesn't even tell Mary, she just gets in Larry's car and drives to where Joshua is. Now that she knows he is coming, she can't wait anymore to talk. She pulls into the rest stop and there they are, lounging in the grass, leaning up against their cars before they come to pay their respects. She walks up to him, her lower lip trembling, trying not to burst into tears and she says, "Where were you?"

No one says anything. They stare at her. Some of them move away, but the teacher keeps his eyes on hers. He reaches for her but she flinches. He pauses, keeps his distance. "Where were you? If you had been here my brother wouldn't have died."

The memories race through her mind:

A girl with twisted legs like sticks of firewood, danc-ing after Joshua's touch.

A crazy, demon-possessed man dressed and well-groomed and sane after Joshua says a few words in prayer.

That ambulance, the back door wide open and the happy victim hugging the paramedics, falling on his knees before Joshua, laughing and crying at the same time.

"Even now," she says, "even now I know that God will give you anything you ask for."

He puts his hands on her arms, and when she looks down, he stoops to keep his face in front of hers and says, "Your brother will live again."

She knows this, of course. Everyone knows this. One day, all of God's people will be brought back to life, to live with him forever. They call it the resurrection, the moment when those who are lying down rise up again forever. But that's not what she's talking about, and he knows it. "I know my brother will live again on the last day."

His warm eyes keep watching her. He won't let her look away. Her jaw is flexing, almost popping, and she's doing everything she can to keep it together. And then he says, "I am the resurrection and the life. Those who believe in me will never die, and those who believe in me will live even if they die. Do you believe?"

"I believe that you are the savior of the world," she says, "the one who was promised to us."

"If you believe, you will see God's glory," he says, and he rubs her arms. Then he asks for Mary.

Unanswered Questions

Mary can't stop sobbing. Her throat hurts, her chest aches, she can't sleep, can't speak for more than a sentence or two before the crying starts again. She sits in the high-backed chair in Larry's room, looking at his empty bed, letting the sunlight move across the bed, the floor, coming eventually to her legs. She's wearing sweats and a T-shirt and hasn't done her hair or her makeup, which would just end up smeared down her cheeks anyway, and she doesn't care that all the family friends have come over, doesn't care how she looks or how she sounds.

Martha lets herself into the room and closes the door behind her and says, softly, "He's at the rest stop outside of town and he's asking for you." Before she can say anything else, Mary leaps up and runs for her purse, fumbles for her keys, doesn't stop for a jacket or her shoes, and pushes her way through a crowd of mourning friends.

He's waiting for her right where Martha said he would be, and when she sees him, she dashes out of the car, not pausing to close the door. She can barely make it across the parking lot; her legs are giving out from under her, and she crosses the sidewalk, collapsing at his feet. She puts her head against his knees, grabbing his legs, leaning against him, sobbing. She chokes out the words, "Sir, if you had been here, my brother would still be alive."

She is vaguely aware of her friends and family, who must have followed her here, getting out of cars, and when they see her, they begin to cry also. He brushes the hair out of her face so he can see her, and his face is creased with concern. He's troubled, deeply troubled. In almost a whisper he says, "Where did you bury him?"

Her friends start back toward their cars, holding each other's arms, wiping at their faces. One of them says, "We'll show you."

He doesn't follow. It's like his feet are rooted, like they're encased in concrete. She stops to look at him, to see if he's coming, and then she notices his shoulders shake. Silent tears course down his cheeks. He's wiping at his face, gasping. They all stand there, staring at him. Finally, Mary takes his hand and pulls him toward the parking lot. *He needs to see the grave to know it's true,* she thinks. *He needs to realize what has happened so he can grieve.*

She's walking with him to the car, and he can barely see. He's holding onto her sleeve. As they walk by one of her friends, she hears her say, "Look how much he loved Larry!"

But another one says, "He can heal blind people. If he loved Larry so much, why wasn't he here to help?"

She wants to snap at them to be silent but she doesn't have the strength and, honestly, it's the same question that she has. If he loves them (and she has no doubt that he does), wouldn't he want to heal Larry? And if he's powerful (and she knows that he is), couldn't he have stepped in and done something? So she says nothing, and the teacher slumps into the passenger seat, and his followers pile into various cars and follow her to the graveyard.

11

Bring Out Your Dead

I met a billionaire once, someone who could literally, on a whim, purchase anything she thought would make her happy. She could purchase a new home in any corner of the earth, give money to charity, start a new career as a hobby. But she couldn't bring her father back from the dead.

I met a girl who lived on the streets of Portland whose boyfriend left her when he found out she was pregnant. She had dark circles under her eyes and track marks on her right arm. Two months pregnant, strung out, living on the street.

I saw a man screech up onto the sidewalk in his sports car, jump out, grab his teenage son, and hit him multiple times in the head before bundling him into the car, yelling the entire time.

I've heard of grade-school girls sold into sexual slavery. I've seen reports of children conscripted into armies and taught to maim, kill, and rape.

I know of horrific examples of abuse in families, stories that make my skin crawl, make me furious, make me jump

125

out of my chair and vow to make things right. There is war, and there are unloved women trapped in horrific marriages and unloved men lashing out at the world around them. The world is full of pain, some of it avoidable, some of it caused for the momentary pleasure of another person, some of it the result of natural forces that move uncaringly across human life, snuffing it out.

Where is God in the midst of all this?

How can he let us suffer?

How can he let us harm one another?

Does he love us?

Does he have the power to change things?

Is he standing by, wringing his hands, shrugging apologetically as we go through the worst moments of our lives?

In John 11 Mary and Martha were asking questions like these. Their brother, Lazarus, had fallen seriously ill. They probably weren't too worried, because they had a close family friend who gave sight to blind people, cast out demons, and held dances for people who used to have crippled legs. They knew he had power. They knew that Jesus loved them. The Bible says this specifically: "Now Jesus loved Martha and her sister and Lazarus" (John 11:5).

So it must have been a shock when they sent news to Jesus, saying, "The one you love is sick," and he didn't reply.

Where was he? Why didn't he show up?

I've asked this question too. After our second daughter, my wife and I went through a series of miscarriages. The pain of losing our third and fourth kids hit me far more deeply than I expected (I've written about this more extensively in my first book, *My Imaginary Jesus*), and I remember praying one day and saying, "I know you're good. And I know that you love me. How could I possibly question either of those things after my experiences with you? I know that you could have intervened. So *where were you when my baby was dying?*"

On the scale of human suffering, a couple of miscarriages may seem like a small thing. The world is full of horrific things on an unimaginable scale. I can barely stand to watch the news, to hear what is happening in other parts of the world or even sometimes right down the street from my house. But one of the great unifying truths of the human race is this: we all experience loss, pain, heartache, death.

During my own grief at the time of our miscarriages, the story of Lazarus was the one that comforted me, because in this story someone asks God, "Where were you?" and he answers the question. He answers it in a variety of ways. He answers with questions and reminders and action. Of course the most memorable, the most powerful moment was when he followed Mary and Martha and their friends into the graveyard, past the monuments and memorials to thousands of years of death, past the flowers and dead grass, past the gates that keep the dead in and the living out. He followed them past the places of easy answers and into the place of absolute despair, into the deepest question in our hearts, the question that is also a prayer: *Oh, God, why have you deserted me?*

The House of the Dead

They wind their way into the cemetery, past the wrought-iron gates and the well-dressed mourners. She parks the car and they walk through the perfect grass and the tall white stones and the wilted offerings of flowers until they come to his grave. Flowers are piled around the freshly churned earth. Ribbons on the flowers declare

Larry a "Beloved Son and Brother." The dates of his beginning and his end, stamped on a temporary grave marker, attempt to make his life something memorable, something permanent. But nothing is permanent, nothing lasts. Not this marker, not the gravestone, not Larry.

Martha is standing there with an armful of flowers to add to the sea of color around his grave. The teacher sinks down to his knees in front of the grave and rests his head on the ground. He stays like that for some time. No one dares go near him. When he straightens, they all watch him expectantly. He turns to one of his followers and says, "Dig him up."

Martha gasps. They all do. He is mourning, of course, and probably doesn't know what to say. Martha speaks up first and she says what they are all thinking, "He's been buried for four days. He's just a corpse now."

The teacher nods. "Didn't I tell you that if you believed, you would see the glory of God?"

One of his followers goes off to find a groundskeeper, who refuses to give them a shovel or anything like it, so they wait while one carload of his followers goes to buy some at the hardware store. Joshua stands over the grave, tapping his fingers impatiently against his arm and then pacing around the stone, again and again.

Twenty minutes later they're back and they get to work, digging out the freshly churned soil. The teacher stands beside them, not talking, as they take turns with the shovels, jumping in as the hole gets deeper until finally there is the sound of metal biting into the sound of metal biting into the cement grave box. The men cleared off the dirt, and at a command from Joshua lifted off the stone lid. Soon after that the top of the casket is clear and the men are out of the grave.

The teacher clears his throat and says, "Father, thank you for hearing me. I know that you always do. I'm just saying it out loud so that everyone here will believe that you sent me."

Then he bends over the hole and shouts, "Larry, come out of there!"

A creaking comes from the hole, and Mary moves close to the teacher, clutching his shirt. The coffin lid moves, then falls back. It shakes, as if something was hitting it from inside, the soil on the lid bouncing, dancing toward the edges, and then the lid flies open. Larry coughs, wipes his eyes, and sits up. Someone screams. One of Mary's friends collapses in the grass. Everyone is staring or shouting or throwing their hands over their mouths.

Larry steadies himself using the dirt walls of the grave. He looks up at the teacher and Mary and Martha and gives them the most dazzling smile. His suit, which had been cut down the back to get it on him, flaps down the front, and he gets tangled in it, trying to get it off without losing his modesty. Mary can't say anything. No one has said one coherent word yet.

Then the teacher looks around, as if someone has missed their cue. His lips twitch into a smile and he says, "Someone get those funeral clothes off him. And get him out of that hole."

Two of his men slide down into the hole and steady Larry. Five minutes later he is standing in front of them, wrapped in a jacket and too-large jeans from someone's car, barefoot and grinning and enveloping Mary and Martha both in his arms. Larry smoothes Mary's hair and kisses Martha on the cheek, and the teacher stands nearby, leaning on the tombstone, grinning.

"We were so scared," Mary whispers.

"Of what?" Larry asks.

"That he wouldn't be here in time," Martha says.

Larry laughs. "He's always on time. Whatever happens, he's on his way."

"But what if that's not enough?"

Larry takes their hands and they march toward the car, the cuffs of his pants dragging in the grass. Every five steps he stops to hitch up his jeans. "To know he's on the way is enough for today, my dears. Let tomorrow worry about itself. Now let's eat. I could die I'm so hungry!"

Your Brother Will Rise Again

I remember a funeral where a friend of the deceased stood in the back, leaning against the pew in front of him, sobbing so hard he couldn't stand. People stood on either side of him, holding him up. I can imagine him asking Jesus, "Where were you when my friend died?"

Jesus says, "He won't be dead forever."

That's the first thing Jesus said to Martha, when she asked him why he hadn't saved Lazarus. "Your brother will rise again."

This is an answer, ultimately, about hope. He was reminding her that, yes, Lazarus was gone, but in time God would bring them together again. He was reminding her that at the end of history, all of God's people will live in community with him and one another. He was saying, "Death is only temporary, Martha."

One day God will make everything right. In the book of Revelation (21:3–4 NLT), an angel comes and makes this pronouncement: "Look, God's home is now among his people!

He will live with them, and they will be his people. God himself will be with them. He will wipe every tear from their eyes, and there will be no more death or sorrow or crying or pain."

God will wipe away the tears that come from the pain that we experience *in this life*. He won't shrug off our losses. He will let us express our pain, our suffering, and he will comfort us. And after that, there will be nothing to cause us tears again, not ever, not for all eternity.

All that is lost will be found. All that is broken will be repaired. There will be no more children on the street, no more parents abusing kids, no more war, no more poverty, never again.

"Your brother will rise again."

It's a reminder that today is not the end of history, that when we walk around our neighborhoods and cities and battlefields and graveyards, this is not the end of the story. In time God will abolish death. In time we will see our loved one's face again.

Martha told him she knew this, that on the last day Lazarus would rise again, and Jesus corrected her. The resurrection is not merely an event. It's not only some moment in the far-off future. He is the resurrection. He is the life. And those who believe, those who have a relationship with him, will never die, no matter how it may seem. The resurrection is a person, and he's already here.

The God Who Weeps

Jesus doesn't spout this off as a platitude. He's not clapping Martha on the back and saying, "You shouldn't cry at a funeral if you believe in Heaven."

The truth is, when Jesus sees Mary and her friends mourning, he is "deeply moved in spirit and troubled" (John 11:33) and he too begins to weep. There are many opinions about why Jesus is weeping at this moment, from anger at the reality of death and its tyranny over humanity, to pain for our loss, to frustration that Mary and her friends honestly don't get it, don't understand that he truly is God and the one who was sent to save the world.

We could argue endlessly about the precise reason that Jesus cried, but frankly, trying to pin it down to one thing seems ridiculous. Most of us don't cry about only one thing. With the same tears we cry about loss and pain and missed opportunities and tiredness and frustration and fear. Why should his tears be simpler than ours?

What does seem clear, however, is that the impetus for his tears is empathy and compassion for us. It's Mary's mourning that sets him off. It's seeing the grief of Lazarus's friends that starts the tears brimming over in his eyes.

Too often I have a picture of an impassive God, standing over creation and being neutral or even pleased by the horrors of the world. But Jesus shows us that's not the case. Jesus sees our suffering and he weeps. He experiences sorrow and loss when he sees us—his loved ones—experiencing sorrow and loss. Then he invites us to tell him all about it, to show him the depths of our pain. After that, in time, he shows us the glory and the power of God.

We're Going to Fix This

So often when we encounter modern-day slaves or the poor, the mistreated, the disempowered, the abused, we tell Jesus the same thing Martha and Mary did. "If you had been here, this never would have happened."

And Jesus says to us, "One day you will be in the presence of the Resurrection."

Jesus asks, "Do you believe that I am the one who has been sent to repair the world?"

Jesus says, "I am alongside you, my arm around your shoulder, crying with you because this world causes so much heartache."

Then he says, "But we're going to fix it."

I've talked to people who have walked away from Jesus because they can't serve a God who allows this much suffering in the world, and I understand that point of view. I think they misunderstand what Jesus is saying but I get the compelling reason they walk away. If Jesus were allowing the world to be this way because he disliked us or because he was impotent to change it, I would walk away myself.

But that's not the case. He is the one who came into the world to fix it. To change it. To save it. My question shouldn't be, "Where were you?" or "Why didn't you?" but rather "How long?" How long until you set everything right and bring justice? How long until your peace fills the earth like an ocean?

Indeed, the injustice and suffering pervading the world are unacceptable. But I don't follow Jesus *despite* humanity's suffering. I follow him because of it. I believe Jesus is the one who can bring lasting, permanent change, and I want to be part of that. He is the Prince of Peace, and I want to destroy injustice and death and chaos alongside him, as his coworker and servant. I want to usher in his kingdom, to play a role in bringing about his rule.

In that sense, I don't stand idly by, watching the broken world, shaking my head, clucking my tongue, and saying, "This is another mark against you, God." No. I put my arm around the billionaire without a father, and I comfort her. I help the girl on the street find a place to stay and find a clinic that will give her unborn child medical treatment. I step between the father and his son and I call Child Protective

Services. I help them get counseling. I'm a follower of Jesus, and when people say, "Where was God?" I ask myself, "Where was I?" I'm his representative. When people ask, "Where was God?" God's people should ask, "Where were we?"

And I'm glad that, in the midst of my own pain and loss, he reminds me a day is coming when he will wipe every tear from my eyes.

I'm thankful that he reminds me that the Resurrection is a person, not an event, and as I come closer to him, I experience more of those "resurrection moments."

I look forward to that day when there will be no more pain or suffering or injustice, when we will be in the presence of the Resurrection and the Life, and the prayer "Let your will be done on earth" will be a simple statement of reality. A day when we will all understand—like Mary did, like Martha did, like Lazarus did—the casual ease with which Jesus made the miraculous commonplace. He's the only one who can save us, and in the midst of a world where we're drowning in injustice, over our heads in sorrow, we're shouting out to him, "Please, please, save us now!"

12

Death Triumphant

At a certain point it became all crowds and cheers and people lining the streets for a parade. They entered the city with the teacher sitting on the back of an open convertible, waving to the people while they, in some sort of frenzy, tore their clothes into flags and waved anything they could find at him, chanting for him to save them.

Then the story took an unexpected turn, like the wolf eating Little Red Riding Hood as she walks down her driveway on her way to Grandma's house. Like a conquering hero returning home to a ticker-tape parade after which he's beaten to death by the adoring crowd. Like a romance that starts with the young couple noticing each other across a crowded bus, just before it careens off a cliff.

The teacher was dead.

He Can't Even Save Himself

The best word for what happened when Jesus was murdered is simply this: *confusion.*

One Sunday their teacher is riding into Jerusalem on a donkey, and people are lining the road with their clothes, the equivalent of putting down a red carpet. They don't want the donkey he's riding to touch the ground. They cut down palm branches and wave them, shouting, "Save us now!" The people believe he's the chosen one, the savior of the world who has come to save them from the oppressive imperial rule of the Roman Empire. He's going to kick the bad guys out and install himself as king, reinstating Israel as a nation. And who wouldn't want a king like this one? He heals the sick, and he feeds the hungry. He is good and just and kind.

Along the way, Jesus keeps telling them he's going to die. He's going to be turned over to the authorities and executed. His followers ignore him, argue with him, misunderstand him. When he gets to the outskirts of Jerusalem, he starts to weep, to really come unhinged, his cries echoing off the buildings, and he says how much he wanted to protect them, to bring them into the fold, to take care of them, but they wouldn't have that. Then the people throw a party in his honor as he enters the city limits. How could you think Jesus is about to be killed when everyone is shouting his name?

Five days later the religious leaders hold a heresy trial in the middle of the night. When they burst in during a prayer meeting, they are led by one of Jesus's inner circle, and they handcuff the teacher and lead him away. They debate what to do with him, decide on his guilt, and at sunrise they turn him over to the authorities. Within twenty-four hours there's a public trial, a mob, and an official execution. The world seemed like it was spinning too fast, and rumors and half-truths ravaged the city as this popular, well-thought-of, controversial man went from the toast of the town to the graveyard.

Meanwhile, his followers, who had expected him to become king and save the world, are disillusioned and confused. How could he have saved anyone? He couldn't even save himself. They're regretting all the sacrifices they made to follow a man who claimed to be the Way but turned out to be a dead end.

Trying to put the crucifixion in modern terms is extremely difficult. It's an event high in what the theologians call "particularity." This means, basically, that it's a unique historical event and the more "particular" it is, the more likely that it's not repeatable at another time or place in history.

There are a few things to understand about this particular form of execution. One, it was relatively common. It was the preferred method of execution in the Roman Empire, and the Romans would put slaves, thieves, insurrectionists, traitors, and troublemakers to death this way without much thought. It was both a brutal way to die (people could live for days or even weeks if provided water) and a vivid, official message from the empire: don't cross us or we'll put you on a cross. People groups like the Jews weren't allowed to enforce the death penalty themselves, it was illegal. Only the occupiers, the servants of the empire, could punish others with death. In fact, Jews were much more likely to be executed this way than Romans. Roman citizens had special rights, and their trials, arrests, and eventual punishments had to be carefully carried out.

We see evidence of the tricky situation this created for the Jews in stories like the one where some religious leaders try to trap Jesus by throwing at his feet a woman caught cheating on her husband.

"This woman committed adultery," they say. "So should we kill her like the Bible says or turn her over to the Romans? Should we ignore the Bible and let the foreigners be in charge of our justice?"

The teacher doesn't even look up. He just stoops down and starts drawing in the dirt. He says, "Go ahead and kill her." Almost like he doesn't care, almost like he's not paying any attention. Jewish tradition demanded she be killed by throwing rocks at her until her skull was crushed and the breath had left her body. "Whoever is without sin can throw the first stone," he says.

The woman stays there on the ground, covering her head with her hands and sobbing. The teacher doesn't move to comfort her or shield her, just keeps drawing. Waiting.

Silently, the accusers drift off, one by one, because none of them are innocent. And not only that, but if the law is enforced, if they follow it perfectly, most of them would be at the teacher's feet, with someone else throwing stones at their skulls. You could receive the death penalty for heresy, for adultery, for disrespecting your parents, for any number of things.

The teacher looks up and sees that the men are all gone. Perhaps he notices that there was not an adulterous man thrown at his feet alongside the woman, and it seems that might have been necessary for this particular sin. Perhaps he recognizes that she is, essentially, a victim that the religious people were using as a political pawn, using her difficulties in life as a way to win a religious argument.

He looks at her and says, "Where are all your accusers? Is there no one left? Didn't they find you guilty?"

No, they didn't find her guilty. Or at least no more guilty than themselves.

"Then I don't find you guilty, either," he says. "You can go home now."

As she stands, he grabs her hand, and she looks down into his brown eyes. "It's time for you to stop making the wrong choices in life. Live life correctly from now on."

Jesus found the woman innocent because her accusers were not. But who is there to stand up for Jesus when he is accused? Everyone runs. The religious leaders decide to get him taken care of officially, so they march him to the Romans. The story gets a little complicated here, as the local officials don't want the political heat associated with Jesus's case and they start sending him back and forth. They can't find any legal reason to kill him. But in the end the mob is so demanding, the politics of the whole thing so messy, that the sentence is handed down. Jesus is innocent and he will be executed.

So the crucifixion is this strange moment when the execution is also a murder, when the mob has a stronger voice than justice, but the official seal of approval from the state is on the paperwork. I racked my brain trying to find a similar practice today, a barbaric murder as an example to others, a mob-induced, public murder with most of a city standing by and approving. It's not the slow-moving stone gears of our justice system, where a guilty man can be let free on a technicality or held in prison for years while we make absolutely sure he's been treated correctly and is in fact guilty. Despite the flaws in our system—the inherent preference for the wealthy, the likelihood of certain ethnicities receiving more punishment than others, the immense slowness—our system is ultimately not as brutal as the Roman system when dealing with a noncitizen. Accusation, sentence, and penalty were all doled out in less than twenty-four hours.

The crucifixion was, in the end, much more like a lynching. It was like a lynching when the mayor and the police force agree to string up the rope.

Mob Rule

Joshua, the teacher, stands on the mayor's wide garden balcony, the place where he often receives official visitors. All the pastors and theologians are gathered there, trying to convince the mayor that this man—this skinny, young man with the tangled hair and the unimposing presence—is somehow a threat to the government. They say he's claimed that he's going to burn down their church (and rebuild it in three days), that he's going to take over the government and rule. The young man doesn't help his case much. When the mayor says, "Do you think you're their king?" he shrugs and says, "You said it, not me."

The mayor asks him what he has done, and the teacher says only that his kingdom isn't of this world, or his people would fight to protect him. But they haven't. His kingdom, he says, is—at least at this time—in another place. The mayor is enjoying himself a bit, and he says, "Aha! So you *are* a king!"

"You're the one who keeps saying that," the teacher says. "I came into this world for one reason: to tell people the truth. Everyone who belongs to the truth listens to me."

The mayor laughs. "What is truth?"

But the teacher doesn't answer his question. Actually the young teacher has never answered any of his questions, not directly. Nevertheless, he doesn't appear to be guilty of anything other than being an annoying conversationalist. The mayor has seen this sort of political maneuvering by his citizens before, so he's not taken in by it and he's not going to fall into a trap. He tried to argue that the teacher falls into another person's jurisdiction but the mayor of the next county over does little more than send back a joke: he dresses the teacher in a silk tuxedo along with a note pinned to his back, "Look! The King of the Jews!"

"I'll have him punished and released," the mayor says, and he has his guards fall on him with billy clubs. The teacher crumples under their blows like a flower in a storm, and when the mayor holds his hand up and shouts, "Enough!" it's clear the teacher has received more punishment than he deserves. But by now the mayor's mansion is surrounded by a mob, all of them shouting for this teacher's blood and it's clear that, if he doesn't hand him over, they'll tear the wrought-iron fence posts from their moorings and advance on the house. He's not afraid to make unpopular decisions but in this moment it's not worth it. What's the life of one homeless, wandering philosopher when weighed against the demands of his office? Nothing. So he writes the decree, and liking the joke pinned on the back of the tux, he gives orders for that particular phrase to be nailed to the tree along with the teacher.

13

The Lynching at Skull Hill

Officer Wilson gathers the rope. Long rope, coils and coils of it, a bundle as thick as a man's arm. There's a ladder, also, a tall ladder that one man can barely lift, and they put it on the shoulders of the handcuffed teacher. Joshua shouts in pain when they lay it on him. The officers make a way through the rabble, and the teacher descends to them, stumbling under the weight of the ladder. People are shouting and jeering, throwing mud, throwing insults.

They're nowhere near the edge of town before it's clear that the teacher cannot carry the ladder any longer. Blood seeps down from his hairline and into his swollen black eyes, caking his cracked, split lips. He scarcely looks human and he's breathing so heavily and falling so often that Wilson is concerned he'll die on the street. Then he'd have to get an ambulance to scoop him off the pavement. Officer Wilson can't allow that, so he conscripts a strapping young man on the side of the crowd to carry the ladder. He doesn't ask, he demands, and with a groan the man falls in step behind them, the teacher stumbling still, his wrists chafing from the handcuffs.

They get him to Skull Hill just as two other lynchings are about to start. Thieves. But the center tree is for Wilson's prisoner, and it's a big, hearty oak, with the lowest branches fifteen feet from the ground. He orders the ladder laid against the tree, and he throws the rope himself, a strong throw that sends the heavy coil up and soaring over, bringing it crashing to earth at the teacher's feet.

His men are having some fun, striking the prisoner and shouting, "Hey, if you're God's messenger, tell us who hit you."

The crowd loves it. A little pageantry. Wilson likes to use the long ladder that the prisoner carries to get the rope up into the tree, but he has a shorter ladder he uses for the prisoners to stand on, and he has his men set it beneath the lowest branch. The crowd is like one large animal now, undulating and thrashing like a massive snake. People have their children lifted up on their shoulders so they can see. Someone is making his way through the masses, selling hot dogs.

Wilson orders the prisoner stripped. No need to waste the silk tuxedo he's been dressed in, and no reason to leave the man any dignity. What has he done to deserve it? They take off the handcuffs, then pull off the jacket. It's bloodstained around the collar but that's barely noticeable at a distance. The shirt is worse, red and brown where it should be white, but it's still a more valuable shirt than any Wilson has ever owned. His men yank it off, buttons showering the hungry crowd. Then the shoes. The teacher isn't wearing any socks. They pull off his pants, and the crowd cheers. One of the men tears off the man's boxers and he stands there, totally revealed, naked before them, bloody and limp and bruised. He doesn't attempt to cover himself, just stands there, hunched over, as if standing is more work than it's worth. The bleeding under his skin is so bad that Wilson thinks he can see the bruises spreading while he watches.

Wilson shoves him toward the shorter ladder. Someone wings a mud ball over the crowd, and it splatters against the teacher, sends him stumbling forward. Angry and afraid that someone might hit him or one of his men, Wilson sends two goons to push the crowd back a few steps. He wraps the thick cord around the teacher's throat and knots it behind his head. Then he tells him to climb.

Everyone watches him, naked and muddy and covered in blood as he takes each agonizing step toward the top of the ladder. He gets to the next-to-last rung and stops. Wilson yells at him, cursing, until he takes the last step and stands, shaky and off balance, at the top. The prisoner's arms should be just long enough to reach the branch above him, if he stands on tiptoe. And that is precisely as it should be.

Wilson calls his men over and they grab the rope and with a savage yank they pull the prisoner off his feet. His hands go to the rope around his neck as Wilson shouts, "No, no, reach for the branch." The prisoner's choking, his face turning purple before his bloody fingers reach the branch and he pulls himself up, just an inch, just enough to breathe. His bare toes find the edge of the ladder and he walks his toes across it, able to put his weight down for a moment if he's willing to hold his breath. Able to breathe if he pulls himself up.

One of Wilson's men says, "Boss, his hands are too bloody. He can't keep a hand on the branch." He's right. If this guy lasts ten minutes, Wilson will be surprised. He looks at the mob, and they're not happy, not yet, and a bloodthirsty crowd like this one might not get tired of watching him die for hours. He needs it to last as long as possible, so Wilson gets the hammer and some nails and he climbs the longer ladder, the one leaning against the teacher's branch.

The prisoner doesn't seem to know that Wilson is up there beside him, not at first. His bloody hands keep slipping over the bark, but he's still pulling himself up for breath, barely. Wilson puts his hand over the man's hand and yanks it higher, pulls it completely to the top of the branch. The man's eyes open, slowly, and he looks at Wilson. He doesn't know what's coming, but his brown eyes are taking Wilson in, like he's weighing him out, like he's seeing into him. Wilson takes the nail from his mouth—and it's a big one, a long, thick carpenter's nail—and he puts the point directly over the center of the man's hand. He raises the hammer and drives it through the flesh.

The teacher screams, and when he tries to pull his hand away he tears the nail through his hand. Wilson yanks it back into place, cursing, and the teacher's legs are kicking, flailing. Wilson hits the nail again, quickly. Then again. Then again, until it's deep through the man's hand and holds it fast to the tree. He quickly does the second hand, ignoring the man's cries.

Wilson is about to climb down when the man suddenly falls silent. Startled, Wilson looks at the teacher, hoping he hasn't gone into shock or died. He sees the teacher's brown eyes, closer than he expected, staring right at him. "Father," he gasps.

Wilson shakes his head, embarrassed almost. "I'm not your father," he says.

The prisoner shakes his head. "Father," he says. "Father, forgive them. They don't know what they're doing."

"Who me?" Wilson says, and the prisoner nods, as if he's relieved. Wilson looks out over the crowd. "Them?"

He nods again as if to say, yes, all of them. Forgive them. They don't know what they're doing. Don't blame them. Don't hold them accountable. Don't find them guilty of their terrible crime.

Wilson stares at the man for a minute, but the prisoner has closed his eyes. He's doing his pull-ups so he can breathe, and every ounce of energy is going into that. Wilson goes down the ladder, and he retreats to the edge of the crowd and watches, trying to see what they see.

Wilson has seen prisoners scream and beg. He's seen them laugh like demons and ridicule the crowd. He's seen them soil their pants. He's seen them give up and kick the ladder away. He's hung them in their clothes and he's hung them naked, bags on their head or faces to the sky. He's seen them die fast and he's seen them hang on for days. He's dropped them so their neck breaks, clean and fast. But he's never strung one up and seen this. He's never seen someone forgive his killers. He's never seen someone love the frenzied mob or even think of them other than to hate them.

He keeps watching this prisoner as the hours go by— when the second prisoner starts to mock him. When the third prisoner proclaims his loyalty to the teacher, even when they're all dying. The teacher's mother, Miryam, comes. Joshua manages to speak, to tell one of his friends to take care of his mother. Wilson is at the edge of the crowd, listening. Later he hears the prisoner shout, "My God, my God, why have you deserted me?"

Wilson is watching at three in the afternoon when the man shouts, as if he suddenly has the strength of a professional wrestler in a sold-out arena, and says, "Father, take my spirit."

Then he slumps down and dangles, dead. Not like he let go and suffocated, but like he just stopped living. It's like he decided to lay his body aside, to put it down and he went on, somewhere else, leaving it behind like an empty piece of broken luggage. Wilson's men snatch the ladders out from under the other prisoners and they kick and dance and die. Wilson is worried that the teacher is alive still, somehow, that he's faking it because he's never seen someone die quite like that, so he climbs the long ladder with a bowie knife and he slides it right between the man's ribs until he hits the heart, and blood and water pour out of him, pumped purely by gravity. He's dead all right.

They claw out the nails and cut the rope, and the teacher falls to the ground, a pile of meat. Wilson kicks him over and looks at his face. It's swollen and waxy and still. *They don't know what they're doing, he said.* He hunches down beside him, studying his face. *What kind of man was this?*

Then the earthquake starts. The two other corpses sway in their trees, and what remains of the crowd stumbles drunkenly into one another, and the sun goes dark. Wilson looks up, expecting to see clouds, but it's an eclipse. The sky darkens to the point that he can see stars, and although he's not a superstitious or religious man, neither does he believe in coincidences.

One of the man's followers is wrapping him tenderly in a sheet, covering his nakedness, covering his wounds. There are women weeping. Not only women, but men weeping too. They're stroking his hair. They're wiping at their eyes with the heels of their hands. One of the men has his black SUV parked at the bottom of the hill, and they're lifting the corpse, trying to carry it down the path to the car. They're treating his body with respect, with something almost like, almost like what Wilson has seen in church—reverence.

Forgive them, they don't know what they're doing. That's what he said. A cold dread is building in Wilson's chest. Who is this man? Who is he? What if . . . ? He looks at the darkened sky, the stars like the points of spears, the sun black, hidden as if it can't bear to look. Wilson says, "This man . . . he must have been God's son." *Oh my God. What have we done?*

Who Is This Man?

"Who is this man?"

In many ways, this question is the crux of this book. It's Mary's question when she becomes pregnant with God's son. It's Pilate's, the mayor's, question ("Who do you think you are? The king of the Jews?"). It's the question of every person who crosses paths with him, and with rare exceptions, people don't seem to get it right. Peter does, when he says, "You're the savior of the world, the son of God." One of the soldiers at the crucifixion does, when he says the same thing.

Yet many say he's a prophet or a good teacher or a madman.

What can we learn about Jesus from his death? It starts with this: Jesus didn't want to die for you.

Shocking, I know. Everyone likes to tell us that Jesus died for us, that he wanted to die for us, that he loved us so much that he happily walked up the ladder and wrapped the rope around his neck and dangled there while the breath squeezed out of him and, as they nailed his hands to the tree, he gave us a cheery wave and passed out of his body, a wave that said, "Hooray, now you can live forever."

Jesus didn't want to die for me. Or you. Or us. We know this, because in the garden of Gethsemane, when he was praying on the night before he was murdered, he turned his eyes toward his Father in Heaven, the one who had come up with this plan to save the world, and he said if there's any way to let this pass me by, let's do that. I don't want to suffer and be beaten and brutally killed. He was honest with the Father, honest enough to tell him that he didn't want to go out like this.

Jesus didn't want to die for us. But he said to the Father, "If there's no other way, then let's do this," and also, "Let's not do what I want but what you want."

So he didn't want to die. But he did want to save us. He did want to follow the Father's plan. He wanted those things more than he wanted to be spared from suffering. He wanted those things more than he wanted his own life. He didn't want to die but he did want us. He didn't want to die but he didn't want us to die either. He didn't want to die but he loved us so much that he was willing to die so that whoever believes in him can live forever.

The crucifixion scenes of the Bible are light on teaching. Jesus doesn't give long speeches from the cross, explaining to people how they should live their lives. It comes suddenly, unexpectedly, as if at the moment of triumph he raised his hands over his head and someone took the opportunity to staple him onto the cross. We learn about his character in the description of his death.

We see that he didn't try to overcome his accusers when he had the power and strength and even the truth on his side. His accusers said he opposed people paying their taxes, a serious charge of rebellion in the empire, but he didn't defend himself even though that wasn't true. He went silently, "like a lamb to the slaughter." Why? Because to open his mouth was to prove his innocence so completely that he would have been released.

When another prisoner being executed started throwing insults at Jesus, he didn't respond. But when a third prisoner defended Jesus and said, "Remember me when you become king," Jesus responded by saying, "Today you'll be with me in paradise."

When everyone else had given up all hope of seeing Jesus installed as king, this man somehow believed it was still possible and wanted to make sure he had a place in the royal court. Jesus, showing that he was not only the truth but also the life, told the man that he would, indeed, experience life in Jesus's kingdom before the day was through. Jesus knew he had the power to promise people a place in his kingdom.

When Jesus's mother came to the foot of the cross, he used his dying breaths to tell his friend John to take care of Mary as if she was his own mother. He told Mary to consider John her son. Even in the worst of his pain, even as he died, he was thinking of others.

He had power over his own life, and when the time came to die, he simply told God that he was coming home and stopped living.

He never denied being the king of the Jews. He never denied being the savior of the world, or the son of God. After the earthquake and the eclipse, there were those who recognized that Jesus was not some common peasant philosopher, but someone important enough that the universe took notice of his death, that something about the world was not right, that things were being done that should not be done.

It's startling that as his own beloved people chanted for his death, he prayed to God, "Father, forgive them. They don't know what they're doing."

I can't imagine saying that. This is the sort of person Jesus is. As we murdered him, his thought was, *I don't want them punished for this.*

That's beautiful, and it's incredible that his message of forgiveness was not one that he foisted on others and failed to practice himself. If someone wrongs you, he once said, don't forgive them seven times but seventy times seven. Keep forgiving them. Forgive others as God has forgiven you. He forgave sins over and over, even when those sins directly impacted him. Even when they nailed him onto the cross.

What Have We Done?

The idea of atonement is this: Everyone sins. Everyone does wrong things. The paycheck for doing wrong things, eventually, is death. But God the Father loved humanity so much that he sent his son to die instead of the people who deserved the paycheck. Jesus came and lived the perfect, sinless, righteous life and then he died instead of us. We've been saved from destruction and death by his death.

That's not the only thing happening at the moment of Jesus's death, however. Jesus is also showing the universe his power and love, displaying what an amazing person he is to all creation. He's defeating evil powers, he's bringing glory to the shamed, he's healing the broken, and he's revealing his might to those who are afraid. All these things are true.

Jesus died because he came to save the world. The Bible says over and over that Jesus came to save us. That by his "stripes" (the lacerations on his back from the whip) we are healed. That his blood made a new agreement between God and us, so we're no longer attempting to get to God through our good behavior and constantly falling short.

We were broken, and he came to heal us. We were lost, and he invited us to come home. We did the wrong thing, and he forgave us. His message, over and over, is simply that.

What we did is simple. We messed up. We wandered off at the zoo; we got lost in the old woman's kitchen; we ran away from home. He refused to give up on us. When he came to our house, the house of his friends, his beloved ones, we murdered him. God came to us, and we rejected him. Then he looked at us, he took our chin in his hands, and he said, "Your debts are forgiven."

Jesus forgave us for killing him on the cross, this place where "who Jesus is" and "what we had done" came together. He begged the Father to forgive us as we tried to snuff out his last breath. That's the kind of person he is. That's the sort of people we are. And they sealed up the tomb and darkness fell over the face of the earth.

14

A Hitchhiker on the Highway

To be in this car, now, headed away from the city through the pounding rain, was like getting hit in the stomach with a sledgehammer. Yet here they are, arguing with one another about what has happened and how and checking their smartphones for insights, hoping for another text or an update to the police blotter or an article on someone's blog, something that could make sense of it all.

Patrick says it's all a hoax, while Jose simply can't believe it. Jose hadn't been there for every step along the way and he keeps thinking maybe, somehow, they're missing something and Joshua is alive. Because that was the crux of the matter. Somehow in less than a week, the riotous, joyful crowd stopped chanting Joshua's name and started shouting for his blood. The religious leaders and government officials had lined up to give it to them, poured it out on them with scarcely a moment's thought.

"But the body," Patrick says. "Where was the body?"

Their headlights reveal a man on the side of the road, all but obliterated in a sheet of rain, his hood up, one straight thumb held toward them. Jose exchanges a quick look with Patrick and pulls the car over. They can't leave the man out in this spring rain, not the way the temperature has dropped in the last hour. The door flies open and the man leaps into the car, cold air radiating off him, the smell of rain and wet clothing filling the little cabin in a moment. He pulls his hood off, his long hair tangled and soaked.

"Where you headed?" Jose asks.

"Same place as you, I'm sure," the stranger says. They ride in awkward silence for a moment.

Then the stranger says, "Looked like you two were having a pretty intense conversation when I got in. Mind if I ask what's got you so worked up?"

"We've been talking about what happened the last few days in the city, trying to figure it all out."

"What happened?" the stranger asks.

Patrick laughs. "Are you completely out of the loop? It's been front-page news for days. Everyone's talking about it. The internet is buzzing. Have you been sleeping for the last three days? Under a rock?"

"What's going on?"

So they tell him. They both tell their stories, how they heard about this teacher, this healer, this man who appeared to be God's spokesperson, and how they had found him, started to follow him. They talk about his teachings: the story of the lost kid at the zoo and the son who ran away from home. They talk about how he treated wealthy people who came to him and messed-up broken people and the poor and the religious, and how sometimes it seemed like maybe he preferred the broken, the sick, the impoverished. They talk about the miracles, the powerful actions he took as well as the powerful words he spoke. Once he fed more than five thousand people with less food than you could fit on a cafeteria tray. Once he spoke a sermon that drove the crowd into a frenzy. He turned people away, he sought people out, he drove them crazy, and he made them sane.

They talk through that last week, trying to make it all come together in some conceivable whole. They hadn't been there for every piece of it. They'd both been there for the parade, when Joshua and his followers came into town. Patrick describes the moment when the teacher told them to go look for a convertible parked near the outskirts of this small town. They went there and found it, got in the car, and turned the key. When the owner came out, Patrick had said timidly, "The teacher needs your car today." The man had nodded and turned around without another word.

Jose tells about the feast. He wasn't part of the inner circle, but Thom had told him about it. How the teacher washed their feet, just like that dancer had done for him once, how he had stripped down to his underwear and wiped their feet off and how he had given them instructions. "Love each other. I've served you in this way, you do the same for others." And then the mysterious moment where Jude slipped away and told their enemies where the teacher was.

A disagreement breaks out between Patrick and Jose at that moment. What was Jude's motivation in doing this? Jose says money. Patrick says a genuine desire to tip the teacher's hand, to move him toward overt revolution.

Regardless, Jude is dead now. Tried to hang himself from a streetlight by an empty lot, and when he fell from the light, his belly burst open like a wet grocery sack, spilling his guts everywhere. They weren't clear on the timing of everything, but that had happened after the arrest sometime.

When the cops came to arrest Joshua, it was pandemonium. Joshua was praying in the park, some of his closest friends were there, stretched out on benches and sleeping. Pete pulled a gun and nicked some guy in the head with a wild shot, but the teacher stopped him and actually prayed for the healing of his enemy. People ran, scattering in all directions. One of the teacher's friends was in such a hurry to get away that the mob tore off his shirt when they grabbed him and then his sweatpants trying to wrestle him to the ground, and he had streaked away in nothing but his Nikes.

Then came the kangaroo trial for heresy with the religious leaders, followed by a mock court at the feet of the mayor, one that ended with cops beating the teacher with nightsticks, and the teacher dragged to a cell.

Everyone scattered.

Even Pete had finally left the teacher, and when Pete told them the story, he was weeping, because when the religious leaders had asked if Pete was there for Joshua, he had denied it, hidden it, cursed at them for trying to associate him with the teacher. And who could blame him? Joshua was supposed to be taking office in a massive landslide vote but instead he was in a holding cell, living under a death penalty.

They beat him. They mocked him. They murdered him. One of Joshua's followers had collected the body and laid it in his own crypt. But he was dead, suddenly and unexpectedly and irrevocably.

But then two of the women went out to the graveyard with flowers Sunday morning and they found the cement door of the crypt tossed off. Two unusual characters, angels some said, told them that the teacher was gone, that he was alive. The women couldn't believe it (but they did) and they stumbled into a meeting of Joshua's followers babbling and half coherent. Pete ran to his car and John to his and they raced like dragsters to the graveyard. Pete was ahead of John at first, but John sprinted past him at the end, and Pete came in to find John lying outside the broken crypt, his hands over his head, panting. Pete ducked inside to find the teacher was gone, the suit they had buried him in empty on the cement slab.

"We don't know what to think," Patrick says, his eyes on the road ahead.

"We're overwhelmed and we're trying to figure it out," Jose says. "Who has ever heard such a fantastical story?"

The stranger in the back listens, squeezing water out of his hair. With both hands he slicks his hair back and then shakes his head. Almost to himself he says, "You fools."

Their eyes widen and Patrick looks in the rearview mirror while Jose turns around to see the hitchhiker. "Your hearts are dull and slow to believe everything God's spokespeople have already told you. Don't you realize this is exactly what had to happen, the precise thing the Scriptures say about the one who would come to save all humanity? He had to suffer before his glorious triumph."

And he starts to lay it out for them, like they're children, like they're in Sunday school. He shows them how the ancient Scriptures, more than a thousand years old, spoke clearly and unambiguously about these events, events they witnessed. A strange feeling descends on them, to think that a thousand years ago, even five hundred years ago, someone looked into the future and saw them. He starts at the beginning, the very beginning, and shows them how God promised that the world would not remain broken forever, but that he would send a savior.

Then the hitchhiker walks them, step by step, book by book, prophecy by prophecy, through a sort of backwards biography of the teacher's life, a biography written before he was born. It included where he would be born, things he would say, a story about his family on the run from the government. It told about people's response to him, about his purpose, about miracles he would perform and the way he would die—in fact it included that in some detail. They had never noticed this before, but as the stranger explains it, they marvel that they hadn't seen this more clearly. Jose follows along, scrolling through verses on his smartphone, peppering the stranger with questions.

Then he explains the resurrection. The fact is, he says, that Jose and Patrick and everyone should have expected the teacher's body to disappear. Not only is it in the Scriptures, but hadn't the teacher himself said this more than once? They had thought he was using a metaphor, but could it have been a statement of literal truth?

When he explains the resurrection, he does it completely by quoting songs, songs they had been belting out in church for centuries. Songs they had learned when they were children, that were tattooed on their brains, the sorts of songs that rise, unbidden, when washing the dishes or walking down a stairwell. "God won't allow his Holy One to see decay" and "I won't die. I'll live and tell of God's works."

They pull into a motel, bleary-eyed and road weary at two in the morning. The stranger thanks them for the ride and starts to walk toward the highway, but it's two in the morning and they beg him to wait to continue his journey until morning. It's not safe to keep going. They offer to get him a room, to buy him a meal at the all-night diner attached to the motel.

Finally he agrees to stay, and they settle around a molded plastic table with molded plastic chairs and they order some food and he tells them more about what the Scriptures have to say about the savior of the world. They continue to question him and each other and they're amazed by the detail of the whole thing. Scripture tells how he would teach and how he'd receive a criminal's sentence, how he'd be buried in a rich man's grave, how he'd be beaten, and how he'd be stabbed in the side.

The food comes, three steaming plates of it, and before they eat, they ask the stranger to pray for the meal. He's clearly a wise man, a teacher, and as he prays, there's something about him, something about his voice, about his words, that makes Patrick open his eyes slightly and look at him through his eyelashes. Then Patrick raises his head and suddenly he recognizes the stranger.

Startled, Patrick makes a noise more like a shout than a gasp. He knocks his chair back and it skitters across the floor like a frightened animal. Jose jumps to his feet too, and their three plates wobble on the table like the last stuttered steps of a spun coin. The teacher's chair is empty.

Hardly knowing what he's doing, Jose walks to the other side of the table, looks under it and then under the chair, as if the teacher could be hidden beneath it, like a piece of gum. Patrick throws some bills on the table and they sprint to the car, Jose spinning around, looking on the roof, beside cars, behind the newspaper dispenser.

Then they're speeding on the highway, hurtling through the darkness and Patrick says, breathless, "Did you feel it? Did you feel it? Did your heart catch fire while he was talking to us?"

Jose knows exactly what he means. His heart is expanding and contracting and it feels like a bright comet's tail of light must be coming from his chest, trailing behind them as they shoot like a flare back toward Joshua's followers. Because they have to tell them and they have to assume that's where he'll go next, that's where he'll be, and as the sun pours light onto the city, they burst into the attic room where everyone has been meeting, and before they can even say a word, someone grabs them and says, "It's true! He's back and he spoke with Pete!"

Thom locks the door, and they start to tell their story, their words tumbling over each other as they explain the hitchhiker and his compelling teaching and how he disappeared. They can't believe it. Everyone is babbling, sharing opinions, shouting to be heard over one another.

Then, as if the locked door was nothing more than a thick fog, Joshua stands there among them.

The Final Lessons from the Savior of the World

I love this scene. It reveals Jesus's sense of humor. He appears alongside some of his followers on the side of the road,

162

followers who are trying to figure out what's happening. They thought he was dead, but now some of their friends are saying that not only is his body missing, he's alive! So Jesus walks alongside them and lets them tell him all the rumors about his death, the whispers of his resurrection. He doesn't tell them who he is, not at first, but instead starts explaining the Bible to them, walking them through the verses that explain everything that would happen: his death, the resurrection, and many, many other things.

They must have been surprised by his knowledge and the power of his words to shed new light on old truths. Like opening your safe and discovering that it has not only a thousand dollars inside but also a diamond necklace and a few gold bars.

He started at the beginning, showing them how, at the same moment that humanity broke it, God had promised to send someone to fix the world.

He showed them how Isaiah 40 described his cousin John, who would come before him and announce his arrival.

He showed them how Psalm 78 said that the savior would teach in parables.

He showed them how Isaiah 29 and 35 promised that when he arrived he'd heal the blind and the lame.

And on and on, he showed them that

the savior would come through the city gates to cheering throngs, riding on a donkey (Zech. 9:9),

his own friends would betray him (Ps. 41:9; Zech. 13:6) and the Scriptures foretold the precise amount of money the betrayer would receive (Zech. 11:12),

he'd be silent before his accusers (Isa. 53:7),

he'd be spat on (Isa. 50:6) and that he would die surrounded by criminals (Isa. 53:12),

he'd be pierced through the hands and feet (Ps. 22:16), and

he would never let death hold him back and he would return from death (Pss. 16:10; 30:3; 49:15; 118:17).

That's only a small number of the prophecies he could have explained to them as they walked along the road. There are hundreds of them, telling everything, from where he would be born to how he would die.

It's fascinating that after Jesus's resurrection, very little time is spent on his teaching, at least not in the way it had been talked about before. Luke gives only half a chapter to talking about Jesus after the resurrection, and twenty-three and a half chapters talking about his teachings, his birth, and his death. The longest account of what Jesus does after his resurrection is found in the two postresurrection chapters in John.

Jesus spends three years walking with his followers and teaching them and he spends about six weeks after his resurrection popping in every once in a while, saying hello, and teaching his people on a few topics. He teaches them about himself and what had to happen, but that's never systematically laid out in the accounts of his resurrection. He assures them that he's alive, that he's indeed himself, that he's in a body.

And then he shares a very specific teaching, a teaching that all four Gospels share, plus the book of Acts. It's about what he wants them to do, how he wants them to represent him in the world. The whole thing, frankly, is unbelievable. I'm not the only one to think so. Maybe you think that too. Some of the people who followed him found it hard to believe, people who had seen him feed crowds and raise the dead. They might have believed their eyes but they couldn't believe his words. So he stayed among them for forty days, teaching them, reassuring them, instructing them, and gently blowing on the ashes of their disbelief until they started to glow with the beginnings of something brighter, something that would spread and burn and set the world on fire.

15

Unbelievable

Thom is telling them loudly that he won't believe that the teacher has "come back" until he sees for himself. He won't be satisfied with seeing him across a field, in the dark, standing in the shadows. He needs to stick his finger in the nail holes, put his palm on the stab wound in his side. He isn't going to stake his entire life on hearsay. Some of the women have seen him, Pete has seen him, but Thom has not. Why was that? Was this a hoax? Some sort of trick? When Thom devoted himself to something or someone, it was 150 percent, and he didn't do that lightly.

Then Patrick and Jose burst in, babbling, and a chaos worse than dinner at a family reunion reigns as they all crowd around them, eager for more news. People half-asleep are roused from their places in the corners of the room, knotting around them, sharing stories, asking for details.

Thom locks the door behind them. Since the teacher's death, they're not sure if they're safe. He steps back into the group, weighing out their stories, checking them for inconsistencies. How did they not recognize him when they picked him up on the road? How did he "disappear"? He walked on water, yes, but he didn't just disappear. Then he hears a voice behind him—a voice he has listened to for three years—say, "Peace be with you."

He turns, and there he is.

Or his ghost (How did he get into a locked room?). Or something (How is he walking? How is he breathing? What are those clothes he's wearing?).

Everyone is screaming, everyone is scrambling backward, trying to get away from him, and it reminds Thom of that moment on the boat when they saw him walking on the water.

Joshua says, "Why are you frightened? Why do your hearts fill with doubt?"

He steps toward Thom. "Touch me and see."

He grabs Thom's hand. "A ghost doesn't have flesh and blood, as you can see that I do."

Thom's fingers explore the holes in his hands, and he guides Thom's hand to the hole between his ribs. Someone is still babbling about him being a ghost, so the teacher asks for some fish. They bring him a piece of broiled fish and he pops it in his mouth and, with his mouth still full, says, "Does a ghost eat food?" No. A ghost does not.

And then . . . then he lays it all out for them. "This is merely what I told you before, that everything written about me in all the Scriptures had to be fulfilled." Thom feels like something in his mind opens, like a locked door has been taken off its hinges and behind it is an entire library of commentaries about the holy words, and he suddenly understands things he's read a hundred times, a thousand times before. How the Christ had to suffer and die and rise again. How the teacher's life ran along a series of events so perfectly in line with the Scriptures that it's as if his life were an engine and the Scriptures the tracks he ran on.

Thom falls to his knees and says, "My Lord and my God," because he gets it now. The teacher is not an ordinary man. The teacher is not just the savior of the world. He's not just God's spokesperson or even God's son. He is God. In the flesh. To doubt that Joshua had been resurrected, that made sense. No one had ever resurrected himself in all history. To doubt that the resurrected teacher was God, that was folly. Thom makes a decision, there on his knees, to follow him to the death, to go wherever he is told, to do whatever Joshua commands. It's a promise that will take Thom to the ends of the earth. He knows it the moment he makes it.

In the weeks to come, the teacher shows up like this often. His followers are out on the water, fishing. Pete is debating going back to his old life, and the others go along because, believe it or not, Pete is more relaxing to be around when he's working. That morning they see Joshua sitting on the beach by a campfire. They see him because he shouts, "Friends! Have you caught any fish?" which is a joke since no, they haven't.

Ever since they met the teacher, it seems that they catch fish only when he whistles for them. Pete strips to his underwear and jumps into the water. He goes in feet first. Thom assumes this is because Pete thinks he'll walk on the water to the teacher, but he falls in and starts to swim while Drew pulls the boat around and heads for shore. When they get there, the teacher has fish cooking on the coals and he shares them with everyone.

Multiple times he shows up and each time he teaches them the same thing over and over. He told them before it would be good that he was leaving because they would be better off with God's Spirit teaching them. Now he says that he has a job for them. He wants them to tell everyone about who he is. Everyone. He wants them to do it with God's Spirit, not by themselves. He tells them they will have God's authority and his power.

Then when it seems they have understood the message, he takes them up on a mountain and he says it again. After that he prays over them, gives them a blessing, and then, unbelievably, his feet lift up from the ground and he shoots up into the air, past an airliner, and is covered by the clouds.

They stand there, mouths hanging open, until angels prod them in the side and tell them he isn't coming back, not right then. And they are so amazed, so full of happiness and joy that they throw their arms around each other and half skip, half run to their church, singing hymns as they go, and they stay there, praying and singing and waiting for the promised Spirit to arrive.

Jesus Christ Resurrection Day Festival

I happened to be in Asia during Easter one year. I was in a country where the regulations about religion are more restrictive than in the United States, the sort of place where the people would understand the desire to lock a door once all the believers are inside. A few of us Americans celebrated Easter together with a group of Asian college students who also believed in Jesus. We took a boat ride out to an island in the middle of a giant lake and rented out all the rooms in a guest house. When Easter morning came, we gathered in one of the tiny bedrooms with the door locked. We sang a few songs, quietly, and I led them in a short devotional about Easter.

In this particular country, missionaries had named the holiday hundreds of years ago. Instead of calling it Easter, they called it Jesus Christ Resurrection Day Festival.

We talked about why this day matters, why the resurrection matters, and we talked about how in their country there weren't many traditions associated with the holiday. This is a country where tradition matters deeply, and a typical holiday has a lengthy list of restrictions, requirements, and expectations. But not Jesus Christ Resurrection Day Festival—at least, not that any of us knew about. Many of them didn't know any followers of Jesus except for this small crowd gathered in a bedroom on an island, so if the Christian community somewhere "out there" had traditions, we simply didn't know about them.

I told them, "You have a unique opportunity. You can create the traditions for your community. If you were to come up with traditions for celebrating the resurrection, what would they be?"

They shared a few ideas, and I clearly remember three. First, someone suggested that in the same way that other festivals are for family, this should be a day when the followers of Jesus get together.

A second idea was, "Whenever we see someone, we can say, 'Happy Jesus Christ Resurrection Day Festival!' and when they ask, 'What is that?' we can tell them! Why would we want this holiday to be a mystery?"

The third, and my favorite, was, "Every Jesus Christ Resurrection Day Festival we can all go and wander around in the graveyard. Then when someone asks us, 'Why are you wandering around here?' we can say, 'We're looking for Jesus but he's not here!' Why wouldn't we want to tell other people that he is risen?"

What I loved about their ideas is that they (new believers, some of them having followed Jesus for six weeks or less) understood something I sometimes forget. The resurrection is not something to be defended or hidden or embarrassed about. It needs only to be shared, because it is unbelievably good news. It's the center of Christian theology, to the point that Paul says that if it isn't true, Christians should be pitied more than anyone else on the planet.

My friends understood that the resurrection is not something to believe privately, but something that must be shared with others.

The Great Thing Entrusted to Us

Jesus's teaching, after he comes back to life and before he leaves his followers slack-jawed and staring into the sky, is often referred to as the Great Commission. It's not called that in the Scriptures. It's a name we came up with. A commission is an authoritative order. People will say that this teaching of Jesus is his "marching orders" to his followers. That's not wrong but it does lack nuance, and because of that, we've boiled this teaching down to one thing: the Big Command.

And it *is* a command but it's more than that. A better name might be "the Great Commission, the Generous Blessing, the Unbreakable Promise, the Incredible Invitation." That's too long, of course, so I sometimes call it the Great Thing Entrusted to Us. It's a great honor, like being asked to be a godparent or being asked to hold onto a priceless wedding ring before the wedding. Jesus is turning his ministry over to his followers and saying, "Now *you* teach people about God and how to follow him."

Luke says that Jesus appeared in a room with his followers, startling and terrifying them. After he had convinced them he wasn't a ghost by eating some fish, he started to explain to them what had happened. He tells them that the crucifixion and resurrection are things they should have expected if they had been reading the law of Moses, the books of the prophets, or the psalms.

> Then he opened their eyes so they could understand the Scriptures. He told them, "This is what is written: The Messiah will suffer and rise from the dead on the third day, and repentance for the forgiveness of sins will be preached in his name to all nations, beginning at Jerusalem. You are witnesses of these things. I am going to send you what my Father has promised; but stay in the city until you have been clothed with power from on high." (Luke 24:45–49)

He opened their eyes.

First, Jesus opened their eyes so they could understand Scripture. Suddenly, all the prophecies of the savior of the world jumped out at them on the page, in their memories, as they heard them being recited at the temple. They didn't have to receive formal training about all this, God made it clear to them.

There is a sort of spiritual gluttony in the Christian communities of the United States that says that people aren't qualified to serve Christ until they've received training. I understand the well-meaning origins of this mind-set. It's important that people know what it means to follow Jesus well. But too often I meet people who are waiting to follow Jesus's instructions because they think they need more training. I'm a big believer in training and growth in knowledge. I do, after all, write books like this one. I speak at training and Bible conferences. I have a master's degree in biblical theology, I can read some Hebrew and Greek. But those things aren't necessary to tell others about Jesus.

I've talked to people who are paralyzed with fear about talking to others about Jesus. They say things like, "I don't know how to answer all the questions someone might ask." They read five books about answering objections to Jesus or they get a degree or they listen to a million podcasts before trying to talk to anyone.

On the other hand, I know a pastor in Nigeria. He tells me that when he goes to a village and shares the gospel and someone accepts Christ, he makes plans to install that person as the pastor in his community and to leave him with the responsibility of making sure that his village hears the good news about Jesus. Guess how long he stays and trains that new pastor?

Three days.

I asked him, "Is that really sufficient? Is that enough training? How will he understand difficult things in Scripture? How do you know he won't start teaching heresy? Will he be able to take on difficult situations?" My pastor friend grinned and replied, "I believe the Holy Spirit and the Bible will be sufficient for this young pastor. If that's all he has, it is more than enough."

Get training. Be passionate about learning and growing. But don't let your desire for more training become an excuse for not doing what you are called to do today.

Repentance and Forgiveness

Jesus says that repentance for the forgiveness of sins will be preached to all nations. We must keep both repentance and forgiveness in balance as we tell people about Jesus. It's tempting to create a gospel about Jesus that is one or the other rather than both.

The "good news" that focuses purely on repentance emphasizes the evils of the listeners, making sure they know they are sinners, that they are destined for Hell and destruction. It's good news based in judgment; it's good news based in a belief that what people most need to hear about Jesus is that he thinks they are horrible creatures. A gospel focused purely on repentance becomes centered, actually, on human beings rather than on God. It's the "good news" of human depravity, with little to say about God other than "He doesn't like that."

On the other hand, "good news" that is focused purely on forgiveness tends to downplay humanity's need for God. This good news says, "You're forgiven!" but never explains the need for a return to God's way of doing things. What you've done or are doing or are planning to do doesn't matter because God will overlook it. It's a "good news" that says, "God likes you exactly the way you are." It focuses on God but warps who he is. He will, in fact, forgive us. He'll forgive us in ways that are scarcely imaginable. But he is not content to allow us to remain as we are. He desires us to become like him, and that requires both repentance and transformation.

Repentance and forgiveness must be preached together, never apart.

Will Be Preached

"The Great Commission is a command!" I cannot imagine how many times I've heard that sentence thundered from a pulpit and how many missionary endeavors have been launched as a result of the guilt and fear that came from that declaration. The Great Commission is, indeed, a command. But it's also something else. It's a promise.

Repentance and forgiveness of sins *will be preached* in his name to all nations. *Will* be preached. Not *should* be preached or *ought to* be preached or *must be* preached or *you* go preach it. In Luke, Jesus speaks of a simple promise. If every single believer stays at home, surfs the internet, and takes a vow of silence, the good news about Jesus will still be preached. Jesus has entrusted us with the good news, but he doesn't need us to make sure the message goes out.

I visited a missionary friend of mine in a closed country. Amy worked with the college ministry of an organization called Cru. She taught college students about the repentance and forgiveness of sins available because of Jesus's sacrifice and resurrection. One day she sat down with a college student and asked her if she had ever met a Christian.

"Yes," the young woman said. "My father and I are both Christians."

Amy was surprised. She had been serving in this country for some time, and it was not common to meet a national believer. This was, in fact, the first time she had randomly met another Christian in this country. So Amy asked, "How did you become a Christian?"

"Because," the student said, "my father and I both really love the *High School Musical* movies."

"I don't understand."

"We love *High School Musical* so much that we wanted to learn everything we could about it. We noticed that the characters in the movie were praying all the time and we wanted to know more about their religion. Because they are Americans, we knew they must be Christians, so we went on the internet and learned all about what they believed, about Jesus being God and how he came to earth to die so that we could live and how he rose again to show his power over death. And ever since that time, we have been followers of Jesus."

Amy sat back, breathless. "That's amazing." But she still had one question. "I don't really remember there being a lot of prayer in *High School Musical*."

"Oh yes," the student replied. "All the time they are saying, 'Oh my God! Oh my God!'"

So. God doesn't need us. He has *High School Musical*.

God is not wringing his hands, wondering if I'm going to tell others about him, hoping he's not going to have to send some tribe to Hell because of my disobedience. He's already promised that all nations will hear the good news about Jesus and he keeps his promises. He invites us to be a part of it with him, to be his coworkers in telling others about himself.

All Nations

"Repentance and forgiveness of sins will be preached in all nations, starting in Jerusalem." That "all nations" piece matters. It took the early followers of Jesus quite a while to get this through their heads. Peter eventually had a vision in which God drove the point home: stop ignoring people who aren't Jewish. And a man named Paul became the first aggressive missionary to the non-Jewish world. It didn't take long before the church realized that Jesus meant what he said. God has entrusted us with telling the entire world about him, not only our immediate neighbors.

There was a time when Christians in America became so focused on telling other nations the good news that they forgot to talk to people across the street. Now the pendulum seems to have swung the other way, with many churches in the United States neglecting anyone who isn't in their zip code. There are churches without international missions, pastors who don't see value in building a church that accommodates people of diverse ethnic backgrounds, and church growth principles that are focused on the saying "Like attracts like."

Reaching those like us matters. We can and should start "in Jerusalem," the place where we live. But "good news" that is a message only for those who match us culturally, ethnically, financially, or nationally is not particularly good.

Is it harder to reach out to those of different ethnic backgrounds and cultures and languages and nationalities and geographies? Undoubtedly, yes. But if we're not involved in telling "the nations" about Jesus, *we're not embracing all that has been entrusted to us.* That doesn't mean you have to pack your bags and get on an airplane to Lebanon today. But it does mean that if your entire participation in telling people about Jesus involves people of the same ethnicity as you, who speak your language, who live in your kind of neighborhood, then you are missing something vital. Maybe you won't go yourself. Maybe you'll pray or send money or send other people, but to be part of this great thing that has been entrusted to us requires that we go to people who are different. Because news that is only for people precisely like us isn't very good news for most of the world, is it?

You Are Witnesses

So repentance and forgiveness of sins *will be preached* all over the world. I can stay home now, twiddling my thumbs and waiting for heaven to finally get here, right? Well, Jesus also says, "You are witnesses of these things."

Witness is a legal term, and we most often use it in court, with witnesses called to tell the judge and jury what they have seen. We tend to think of it like this: If I see a car wreck, I'm a witness. I can stay home and keep my mouth shut or go to court and share what I saw. If I go to court and am honest, I'm a good witness. If I stay at home and say nothing, I'm a poor witness.

Let's think about it a different way. A few years ago, a friend of mine died unexpectedly. She checked into a hospital for what she thought was a simple headache and she never left that plain white room. She left behind a husband and four kids, the youngest of whom was two years old. Her husband said, "Listen, my kids don't know their mother. You know her, you loved her, and I want them to know and love her too. Would you videotape some stories and thoughts about their mom so when they get older they can watch them and know how amazing she was?"

He was asking me to be a witness. He wanted me to share my own experience of my friend so that her children would grow up to know her and love her. He didn't coach me on how to talk about her. He didn't guilt-trip me into doing it. I was glad to share a couple of stories. I was thrilled to tell the kids about their mom because I loved her and wanted them to know her too.

"Witnessing" about Jesus should be a simple thing. We've made it complicated, adding all these rules, all these phrases that must be said. We want to coach the witnesses.

Take a deep breath. Here is what a good witness does: a good witness tells other people about their experience with Jesus. That's it. Who he is. What he has done. What he is doing. Not because we feel guilty. Not because we're obligated, but because we love Jesus and we want other people to know him too.

Clothed with Power

"Stay in the city until you have been clothed with power from on high." Jesus tells his followers not to leave Jerusalem without the Holy Spirit, whom God has promised them. What's important to note here is that we're not meant to teach everyone about Jesus on our own. God's intention is not that eleven men on a mountaintop go out and, all by themselves, tell everyone on earth the good news about Jesus. That would be impossible. Instead, God works alongside us, through us, and for us by the power of the Holy Spirit. And the Spirit gives us power to accomplish what he has called us to do.

Jesus didn't tell his followers to feed the thousands and then not give them the food to do so. He didn't invite Peter to walk on the water and then let him do a cannonball to the bottom of the sea. He didn't invite us to tell all humanity the truth about who he is and then wipe his hands and say, "I look forward to watching you figure this out." No. He entrusted us with the most important work of creation's restoration and then promised to work alongside us through the Holy Spirit.

All these teachings reveal something about Jesus. He cares about the whole world—every people group, every culture, every "nation, tribe, people and language" (Rev. 7:9). Jesus does miracles but he likes us to be involved in them. Jesus enjoys empowering his people to do things on his behalf.

And he has entrusted us with this beautiful command, this lovely promise that we sometimes call the Great Commission. And the main idea behind it is to tell the lost, the broken, the hurting, the far off what you have seen of Jesus. Tell them he wants them to come home and that all their debts have been paid.

And the response of his followers when they heard all this was not fear or guilt or concern or feeling overwhelmed. Instead, they responded with "great joy" and they stayed continually at the temple praising God and waiting for the Spirit to arrive so they could get to work. I suppose they looked back fondly in the years to come on the excitement and anticipation of those days.

Strange Travelers

Thom sits near the men in their robes, all of them cross-legged on the floor, and he does his best to stumble through the words he has been learning. They are sharing a meal, and the food is strange: strangely colored, strangely spiced, cooked in a way unlike what he was used to at home.

There have been miracles. He has spoken to them fluently more than once. He has healed their sick, of which there are many. He left home and set out in the direction everyone said was the most difficult. Thom chose the path of greatest resistance. When Pete asked him why, he said, "Because the greatest miracles come when we have the least to offer."

Somehow Thom knows that he will die here. These people who seemed so painfully far from God when he first arrived have become dear to him, so dear that the thought of leaving them stabs him like a spear in the heart. He loves the way the women throw the dough against the side of the clay ovens, the way the men walk alongside the cattle, the children running and shouting with their sticks brandished like swords. Although his miracles have caused him to be welcomed in the palaces with open arms, he still feels a great kinship with the common people, with their plain speech and simple lives. They remind him of home.

Every once in a while he tells the story of the teacher and someone stands against him, argues with him, gives the most vicious skeptic's denial. These are the people he loves most of all. Not because they doubt but because when faced with the truth, skeptics become the strongest believers. He has no doubt they will believe in time, because the truth has nothing to fear from inspection. Let them rail and raise their voices and construct their arguments. There is no argument that can explain away Thom's finger in the teacher's hand or the warmth of Joshua's wounded side against Thom's palm.

He tells them the stories again. Even the skeptics enjoy the stories. He begins with the girl writing poetry in her bedroom, and he walks them through the teacher's life. He shares about his marvelous teaching, his inexplicable miracles.

There have been times when he cannot speak about Joshua's death. He has tried to sort out the emotions but there are too many strands knotted together—his own disbelief, the shock at the loss of the teacher, the clarity of hindsight that strikes him with intense force, the remembrance of his return, and the thought, as he watched his dead teacher eat a piece of broiled fish, that he could never be shocked again. Then six weeks later, the shock of watching the teacher rise into the sky after giving them his blessing, the same blessing that had brought Thom here.

"He'll come back the same way," Thom says, and he points to the sky. Some laugh and point to the sky too. Others stare at him with narrowed eyes, trying to discover if he is telling them the truth. Some smile, already in love with this teacher he describes.

One of them says, "Tell us another story. Do you have any we haven't heard?"

Thom laughs at that. "Yes, of course. He did many other wonderful things. If they were all written down I don't suppose the whole world could hold the books that would be written. There wouldn't be enough room on the internet for all the stories."

He pauses and takes a bit of hot bread and uses it to scoop up a morsel of fish. He puts it in his mouth, chewing carefully while he thinks. A wind blows across him, reminding him of a moment he wants to share. They are watching him, leaning forward, eager to hear what he might say. He smiles and begins another story of what he has heard, what he has seen with his eyes, what he has looked at, and what his hands have touched.

And they stay with him until long after dark, gathered around the great light and enveloping warmth of his stories.

Epilogue

We always start with Miryam.

She tells the whole story: the angel, the train ride, the simple poem on lined paper, life swelling inside her on God's command.

She goes on: Joshua at a pastors' conference, the pastors gathered around the twelve-year-old who not only defeats their quizzes but gives answers that shock tears into their eyes, that make them shake their heads and say, "Watch this one. He's going to be the greatest pastor of us all."

She talks about the wedding reception he saved, about her embarrassment sometimes with the way he acted, the way he spoke. One time, right in front of her, he said, "Who is my mother?"

She talks about his execution, how he looked down on her, battered and swollen, and thought of her, made sure she would be taken care of. She used to wonder what kind of man he would be, she says, but now she wonders that a man like him could exist at all. She wonders at his confidence that a whole new breed of human beings—people like him—would come into existence because of his teachings.

Pete tells stories too, starting with hearing the teacher speak in church, inviting him to dinner, how the teacher healed his mother-in-law and then spent the whole night praying for the sick, casting out demons, and teaching. He talks about the moment when he realized this was no ordinary man: when all the fish in the world swam into his boat and sank it, when Joshua stood on the gunnels and told a storm to knock it off, when the teacher called him and said to walk across the water.

Drew teases him for sharing only the good moments, and Pete sobers and shares about the night Joshua died, about the fear we all felt, about the shameful things we all did, how we hid and cowered and shook, hoping not to hear a sharp knock at the door, not to hear sirens on our streets, not to find ourselves in a kangaroo court. Then he tells quietly of meeting the teacher on the beach, days after his death, and how gently the teacher forgave him.

So many stories use that word. *Forgiveness.* Whether they start in skyscrapers or litter-filled, stinking alleys, so many of the stories end with the teacher saying, "You're forgiven." There's this electric desire to share it, to tell other people about this. To show them the constellation of our scars, the chaotic pattern of our wounds, the incontrovertible evidence of our old lives and to say, "You don't have to live that way anymore. He wants you to come home. He wants you to know him, to be part of our family."

We take turns telling our stories, our stories about the first time we saw him, or the first time we heard him speak, the first time we saw a miracle, the first time we knew that we would follow him to the very ends of the earth. This reminds us of our friends who have scattered like dandelion seeds, who fill the world like dye coloring water.

Thom in India.
Matt in Ethiopia.
Mark in Greece.
Nate in Turkey, having just sent word he was heading for Armenia.

At least once a year we meet for a meal and share stories:

The clear-eyed man, no longer blind, who shares his first sight of the world.
The food passed through a crowd thousands of times too large, the meal with more leftovers than the original sack lunch contained.
The teacher pulling open the back door of a hearse and yanking open the casket to reveal a child, healthy and whole.
The night of prayer at the park.
The lynch mob, the court, the execution.

Feminine voices share the story of the rich man's crypt, the cement slab thrown aside, the bars torn off, the empty white marble inside.

We hear stories of a disappearing hitchhiker in the rain. How he appears inside a locked attic among his terrified followers. How he tells us over and over that he is entrusting us with a few things, that he wants us to share our stories—his story—with everyone.

Looking around the table, we start to believe we really could take this story to every corner of every society. There are ancient men and women, people from other countries, other ethnicities. A young Latino man has his arm around an elderly black woman in expensive clothes, who is holding the hand of a white man in torn jeans, and they're all grinning as they tell their stories—the rich and the poor, seated at the table together. There are people with vastly different philosophies, opposing politics, loyalty to different sports teams, and they're all at the table, they're all his followers, all his family.

Paul begins to speak, a relative newcomer, and he tells how he met Joshua while driving between cities. The story involves a blinding light, Paul's car abandoned on the side of the road, and one of our own coming, at last, to pray for him. The teacher, in the midst of that light, asked him, "Why are you hurting yourself by running from me?" Paul doesn't run anymore. He's been beaten by gang members and lost in the wilderness; he has survived plane crashes and now he's setting out again to tell more people about our amazing, beloved teacher.

Miryam begins to cry when she hears Paul's story, and John puts his hand on her forearm. "It's like Joshua never died," she says, choking the words out. "He was born but he never died."

Martha nods and her hand slips across the table to Larry, who grips it and smiles, his other hand on Mary's shoulder.

Pete says, "Wherever two of us get together in his honor, he's here with us." And as he says it, we can feel him, like the weight of air, near us and constant, and we live and breathe and move within him and there is the sudden certainty that, should he choose to do so, he might walk through the wall and take a seat beside us, break the bread, and pray for us.

We can feel him branching out from this room and into the world, his words like a few careful lines of computer code, traveling from computer to computer, spreading across every network, filling the whole world with his presence.

Pete lifts his wine glass. "In his memory," he says, and we toast together, and we drink, and we tell stories long into the night, and there is raucous laughter and there are tears and comforting arms and hymns and on the way home we link arms and hold car doors for one another and there are kisses on cheeks and warm hugs and we tuck into our beds warmed by our memories and, when the sun wakes us, we rise to make another day of memories together with him, here, in the real world, where he lives.

Acknowledgments

To you, the reader, thank you for reading this book. I hope you met with Jesus in these pages and will continue to do so after you close it up again. If you have questions or thoughts, I would be glad to hear from you. Don't hesitate to drop me a note.

Dann Stockton and Greg Horton both told me to write something serious and unquestionably theological. This one's for you.

Marc Cortez let me experiment with early versions of a few stories on his blog, which gave me confidence that this might be worth exploring in book length.

Wes Yoder loved this project from the beginning and helped it grow up into the book it is today. Thank you.

Huge thanks to my editors, Jon Wilcox and James Korsmo, and all the amazing people at Baker Books for the hard work they've put in to create the amazing product you're reading today. Despite what you might have heard, writing and publishing books is a collaborative effort, and I've been glad to work with this team.

Andy Crouch took time to process a difficult story with me and helped me see it through a different set of lenses.

Ryan McReynolds, Bret Ogburn, and the Epicenter conference let me present four stories at their winter conference in 2013. It was a great experience, a lot of fun, and helped shape this book. Thank you.

To all the students, staff, and friends at Big Break, thanks for the many opportunities to talk about Jesus and the space to share conversations about why he matters to us today.

Enormous thanks to Shasta Kramer, who listened to stories multiple times, processed ideas with me, and gave invaluable feedback along the way. You continue to be my most dedicated first reader, and I'm very thankful for your insights.

The StoryMen, JR. Forasteros and Clay Morgan, have listened to me talk about this book ad nauseam and have given more than their fair share of encouragement and laughs along the way.

Many thanks to Dr. Mary, who gave me great insight into the parable of the lost sheep and allowed me to steal one of her life stories to share with my readers.

To my excellent wife, Krista, and my dear children, Myca, Allie, and Zoey, who have to flex and live life with a book as if it's a member of the family, thank you for your patience and kindness throughout the process. I love you. What book shall we work on next?

Special thanks to Doug Stolhand, who, at a key moment in my life, reintroduced me to Jesus. And to my parents, who did it the first time around and continue to remind me that he's never far from each of us.